BRAINSENSE SERIES: BOOK ONE

The Best Advice Your Mother Never Gave You:

A Guide To Finding Love in the 21st Century

Cathy Lumsden, M. A.

"The Best Advice Your Mother Never Gave You offers a new perspective in approaching our relationships – whether it is in need of re-vitalizing, rebuilding, or as one enters into a new one. Brainsense makes sense. She provides us with useful, practical guides to work with – and this puts the reader back in the driver seat."

Dr. Judy Chow, *MD.*

"This book's finest message is that awareness of your old patterns and behaviors is the cornerstone to healthy relationships. The Best Advice My Mother Never Gave Me is an easy and practical book that every person should read to help them optimize all the relationships they are in."

Alyson Schafer, *The Parenting TV Show; author of Honey I Wrecked the Kids; Breaking the Good Mom Myth*

"There is no question that, for me, Cathy has been a godsend. The death of my husband was interfering with my ability to function at work in everyday living. More importantly, through her gentle probling she helped me realize that my relationship with my husband had protected me from facing up to issues that had been with me since childhood and that his dealth had left them exposed. Cathy brings some very special gifts to her work – warmth, a wonderful sense of humour, deep respect for her clients and the ability to quickly build a sense of trust. With her help I have been able to find a way to cherish my husband's memory while, at the same time, making a start at creating a life without him."

Senior Manager

"I was referred to Cathy Lumsden because I was experiencing a severe depression due to work related and home life factors. I felt that I had lost the balance to my life and that one side of the scale had hit bottom. Cathy was able to use her professional skills most effectively. Through her objective and encouraging therapetutic approach,she provided me with the inner tools to learn to deal with life."

Elementary school teacher

"I have been going to Cathy for a number of years on and off. Cathy was able to gently and successfully lead me to my own answers and help me to accept and make peace with my past. She is a knowledgeable and incredibly competent therapist. I have recommended her to a number of my friends who also found her to be effective in helping them to deal with emerging and difficult life issues."

Fund Raising Campaign Director

"As someone dealing with the frustration of an unknown illness and self-esteem issues, I found sessions with Cathy Lumsden invaluable. By implementing various techniques, from discussions to visualization to EMDR to her Brainsense techniques, her guidance helped me deal with my emotions. Cathy's genuine commitment to using and developing tools to help her patients both during and outside of office sessions is commendable."

Senior Economist

"Listening to Cathy's brainwave entrainment CD is a treat I give myself when I want to relax deeply and feel rejuvenated! The gentle pulsing soothes my tired brain and it feels like my soul is being massaged."

Tanis Day PhD, healer, teacher author of *The Whole You*

"I've had trouble sleeping for most of my life. Anxiety haunted my waking hours and when it was time to rest, it seemed it was open season in my subconscious. By using e-brainsense audios before bed and combining them with a restructuring of limiting beliefs, I was able to quiet the thoughts and feelings raging through my mind. Finally my life turned around."

Business Owner

In loving memory of my mother, Patricia.

She taught me many things, one
of them being the love of books.

Thanks, Mom.

National Library of Canada Cataloguing in Publication Data
Lumsden, Cathy

The Best Advice Your Mother Never Gave You: A Guide to Finding Love in the 21st Century/ Cathy Lumsden

ISBN 978-0-9811616-2-4

1. Relationships. 2. Self-Help.   I. Title.

Cover design: Donald Lanouette

Printer: Lightning Source Inc.

∞

DEDICATION

To my beautiful daughters, Nathalie and Jenna: Their smiles, laughter, and brilliance fill my heart with joy and love, motivating me to follow my life passions and dreams. My hope is that they, too, follow their passions and life purposes, making the world a happier place for all.

ACKNOWLEDGEMENTS

Deep gratitude to my Dad, to Linda, and to my sister Janet and my brother Scott who have been by my side through thick and thin. Your love, encouragement and words of wisdom have been the wind beneath my wings. Feeling your unconditional love and support provided me courage to write this book.

I also want to thank my closest friends, Lori and Andrée. We have shared many years of laughter, learning, struggles, and sorrow. They have assisted me in understanding relationships, listened to all of my "why" questions about partnerships, and were always there to lend a loving hand. I am also grateful for my colleagues, Marion and Susan for our solid and loving friendships.

To my partners in life, especially Brian. They have taught me more than they may ever realize. I am grateful for these amazing individuals. Through my relationships, I have become more aware of my old patterns and behaviors that contribute to unhealthy interactions. I have learned many valuable lessons, strengthening me as a woman, mother, and psychotherapist. In learning these lessons, I was then able to write this book, which I hope will inspire others to seek and create vibrant, healthy relationships. Thank you for all of your gifts and support through our journey together.

∞

Many thanks to those who read my manuscript, edited it, and provided incredible feedback, especially Nancy Peske, Linda Sivertsen, Carole Ann Cole, Alyson Schafer, Joan Oshatz and Dr. Judy Chow.

With warmth, love, and gratitude,
Cathy

Please note: The names used in this book have been changed for confidentiality reasons.

TABLE OF CONTENTS

TABLE OF CONTENTS

INTRODUCTION

"We see things not as they are, but as we are."
—*The Talmud, 200 C.E.*

This quotation from the Talmud is one of the most profound quotes I have ever come across, and it resonates with the underlying premise of this book. All of us view the world, life events, and situations through a set of glasses created when we were very young children. These glasses are basically composed of belief systems, which to a large extent influence our behaviors, emotions and choices. These patterns become etched in our brains and we habitually act oblivious to why we're behaving the way we are.

Beliefs and behaviors that have been passed down from generation to generation are referred to as intergenerational patterns. To best illustrate inter-generational patterns I would like to refer to the commonly known "pot roast" story: One day a little girl was watching her mother prepare a pot roast for dinner. The mother cut off one end of the roast and then the other. The inquisitive little girl asked, "Why are you cutting off the ends?" Her mother replied, "Because my mother did." The daughter was extremely curious and called her grandmother to ask her why she always cut off the ends of the roast. Her grandmother chuckled and said, "Because my roasting pan was too small." The mother was continuing a behavior that she had seen demonstrated by her own mother over many years, never knowing why she was doing it. These intergenerational patterns of behavior in a sense can be called the legacy that has been subconsciously handed down to us.

But like the mother in the "pot roast" story who cut off one end of the roast and then the other, because that is how she saw her mother do it – our mothers are not to be blamed. Mothers are an extremely important and integral part of our society as well as our lives. Without mothers none of us would be here. I admire and am grateful for mothers. I, myself, am a mother to two beautiful daughters and two amazing step-children.

When we were growing up our mothers taught us many important things as far as navigating the world we live in. However, most of our mothers never taught us about having emotionally healthy relationships. Why? Because our mothers were never taught about relationships, nor were their mothers or their mothers' mothers. Plain and simple – in life we do what we know – and many times that ends up being what we learned in our own family dynamics.

This reminds me of a story I read in Linda and Richard Eyre's book, *The Book of Nurturing: Nine*

Natural Laws of Enriching Your Family Life. In one chapter, Richard tells a story about crabs. He grew up in Baltimore and would often go to the seashore with his family. Once crabs were caught and put in a bucket, it was easy to keep track of them because they would "pull one another down." As he explained, if you had only one crab in a bucket, it would get out. If, however, you had two or more crabs, they would never get out because they would continually pull each other back into the bucket. They just do what they know. When I read this story it reminded me of how we humans also just do what we know, like our parents did.

Richard ended his chapter with an encouraging message. Eventually, crabs "shed their hard shells in order to grow." Like crabs, we, too, can shed our old behavior patterns and choose to learn new ones. Awareness of these belief systems, especially the self-limiting ones, is the key to vibrant joyful relationships.

The Best Advice Your Mother Never Gave You is the advice your mother would have lovingly given you – if she, herself, had been schooled and educated in having healthy and loving relationships. But it is not too late to learn these skills and put an end to lifeless, unsatisfying relationships.

I wrote this book as a guide to finding love in the 21st century and it will teach you all the things your mother never knew about relationships and it answers such perplexing questions such as, "Why is my relationship failing?" Many of us ask this question at some point in our lives. We search for the answer in books, counseling, religion or spirituality, and in discussions with friends. Sometimes we find answers and our relationships grow. Other times we find temporary solutions that fizzle out as time passes. Chances are if you are reading this book, you are still searching.

> "I woke up one night half asleep and realized my husband was packing his bags. Instant panic and fear flooded my body. What's wrong with me? Maybe if I had sex more or stopped being so irritable when I had PMS, or paid a little more attention to him this would not be happening."— Sarah, age 51

> "I arrived home one evening after work, and my wife, baby son, and all the furniture was gone. I wandered around the house aimlessly and then sank into deep despair."— Peter, age 35

> "My husband and I are like roommates at college. He sleeps in the guest room and has for five years. We're civil to each other, mainly because of the children. Is this all there is to marriage? How did we get here?"— Rebecca, age 42

"I've been divorced for three years now
and I am petrified about dating or starting
a new relationship. I failed at the last one.
How do I expect to succeed at another
one?"— Simon, age 43

These stories could have come from any of
the millions of people going through divorce or
separation, or living in a lifeless relationship. I
see many clients like Sarah, Peter, Rebecca, and
Simon in my office who are devastated by life and
disillusioned with relationships. Heartache can be
one of the most painful experiences of life. With over
twenty-five years experience as a psychotherapist, I
believe I have found the answer to building and
sustaining happy relationships. Daily, I have the
privilege to witness individuals salvaging their
relationships and discarding their sabotaging behaviors.
I see anger and resentments dwindle away, replaced
with compassion and forgiveness. It became apparent
to me that individuals needed a practical book that
cuts through the confusion of why relationships fail.
People need to better understand why and how we
hurt ourselves and others in relationships, and how
not to continue these behaviors. *The Best Advice Your
Mother Never Gave You* was written to give you
insight and tools to ease confusion and feelings of
loneliness, anger, or helplessness you may have. You
will find yourself changing in ways that will open the
door to love, understanding and communication.

This book is about relationships—the relationships that you have with others and, most importantly of all, the relationship that you have with yourself. We all yearn and dream of acceptance and love from our partners. We all want to know we matter to them. However, we cannot have a healthy relationship with others until we have one with ourselves. But how many of us know how to actually create that? The good news is that it is not as difficult as you may think. But do not take my word for it. Read on and decide for yourself.

I am introducing a new phenomenon called **Brainsense** in this book, the process of becoming aware of your self-limiting belief systems, as well as awareness of your coping strategies that have evolved from these belief systems. Awareness begins with exploring your thoughts and feelings, especially when you have intense reactions. As children, we needed to create coping strategies to deal with our big emotions. However, now that you are an adult, you have the capacity to choose more effective coping behaviors. I know many individuals, including myself, whose old patterns contributed to the deterioration of their relationships, influenced the type of partner they chose, or kept them continually searching for the knight in shining armor, the damsel in distress, or the perfect soul mate. The first step in **Brainsense** is awareness; the second step is exploring and shifting the old conscious and unconscious brain patterns and behaviors. Stepping out of our old patterns and authentically learning how to love ourselves and others is the new way to find love in the 21st century. In the upcoming chapters you will find two self-assessment tools which help you propel the awareness process.

I guarantee that if you or your partner are experiencing emotional reactions that are out of proportion to the situation, you can be sure that your self-limiting beliefs are being reactivated. Or, if you are feeling a lack of enthusiasm for life or your partner, it may also be a sign that you are being hijacked by your limiting beliefs. When your emotions take over, you might find yourself saying and doing things that hurt yourself and others. With **Brainsense**, you can stop reacting in your relationships and start responding. You will learn new ways to handle situations and conflicts with your partner. You will feel the peace of knowing you can control your emotional reactions and communicate lovingly with your mate, yet still be assertive when necessary. You will also come to understand how your mind works and how your thoughts, beliefs, and emotions affect every aspect of your life—your behaviors, feelings and choices.

Need a new way to see your relationship? You will learn five **Brainsense Principles** that will lead you to create vibrant fulfilling relationships. These **Brainsense Principles** will also assist you in developing a new language for building effective communication with your partner. Figuratively speaking, a pair of *Brainsense glasses* is provided, allowing you to observe life through different lenses and enabling you to see yourself and others in novel ways. When you are able to see your relationship through fresh eyes and apply new habits of communicating, your relationship will thrive. Learning to understand and respect each other's differences instead of pushing your point of view fosters tenderness and compassion. I assure you that it will be well worth it to look at your dynamics with yourself as well as your dynamics with your partner in a whole new way.

I suggest that you read through this book once, completing the exercises, and then reread it frequently. Practicing the tools and tips daily will catapult your progress exponentially! You will learn how to catch yourself when you are reacting or overreacting and you will learn how to recognize your old behavior patterns.

This book lays the foundation for taking back control of your mind, your emotions and your life. Byron Katie, author of *Loving What Is,* eloquently states that "Our mind's job is to think, but we don't have to believe everything it says!" We all have a desire to be happy and at peace. However, that intention can become buried by our self-limiting beliefs. The mind stores all our old beliefs and plays them back to us over and over again. You will learn to identify your thought processes that lead to shifting behaviors that no longer work for you. Look out, mind—**Brainsense** is taking over!

In my personal life and my work with my clients, I have seen enough to state my conviction that people have the ability to rebuild and revitalize their relationships. I believe that marital separation and divorce rates can significantly decrease when individuals become aware of their limiting beliefs and coping styles that sabotage their relationships. Once aware of unconscious behaviors, anyone can then choose to act differently.

Many relationships start off on an exciting, passionate note as two people learn and discover each other. These initial stages of infatuation we all go through can be totally intoxicating. You miss your partner when the two of you spend time apart, and ache to have to say good-bye. Then, as time passes, the intoxication begins to subside and your beloved falls off the pedestal. This is often the point when you begin to see your lover's flaws and limitations. Reality sets in, conflicts begin and you are likely to blame your partner for them. After all, were they not the perfect partner just a short while ago? Something you had not noticed before about them becomes suddenly annoying or irritating and you could swear that they are doing it on purpose to hurt you or make you angry. You perceive that they have changed, but did they really? Or is it your perception of them that changed? The relationship is at risk of ending when you are in this power struggle phase. You, and perhaps your partner as well, may hope to find someone who does not fall off the pedestal, but eventually we all fall off. This is simply the growth process every relationship goes through. Fortunately, individuals and couples who use the **Brainsense** process are able to make it through the *falling off the pedestal* stage and see their relation-ship evolve into one in which there is mutual understanding and connection.

Whether you are single and looking for a partner, or you are involved in a committed relationship, this book will help you create a healthy, loving relationship. I just want you to know that not only have I taught these steps to my clients, but I have also taken each and every step myself. I understand the pain and joy of relationships and I have experienced the freedom that using **Brainsense** provides. My fervent hope in writing this book is that you can gain awareness of your behavior patterns, choose to create dynamic relationships, and become your vibrant self.

Shifting old behavior patterns also benefits our children. As parents, we model behaviors and give verbal and nonverbal messages that can be counter-productive to fostering healthy, happy children. Frequently, we are not conscious of these messages—they are habitual, learned behaviors passed down from one generation to the next. The more aware we are of these behaviors, the easier it is to choose different ones to model for our children. Imagine a drop of water hitting a calm still lake, creating a series of ripples. When we shift our old patterns, we create a ripple effect in our families. What a gift we can provide to our children and to the generations yet to come.

With love and gratitude
Cathy Lumsden

CHAPTER 1:
WHAT MOTHER
DIDN'T KNOW

"As long as you have not reexamined your belief systems, and discarded the portions you never actually choose as an adult, you will never fully grow up."

~ Barbara DeAngelis, Ph.D.

Martha sat teary eyed in my office, explaining that her boyfriend recently ended their relationship. She belittled herself, saying, "No wonder he dumped me. I'm so uninteresting and boring and serious. The only time I lighten up is when I drink." Martha felt that she'd finally met the guy of her dreams, after dating for many years and now she had "blown it." At 27, she was a beautiful woman and realistically could pick any man to date. Needless to say, she could not see this about herself. Before the breakup, Martha kept herself busy with mindless activities involving her boyfriend and work in order to minimize her dark thoughts and feelings about herself. Busyness kept her from thinking about how unhappy she really felt. Now that the love of her life had rejected her, the floodgates of emotions were crashing open.

Martha was caught in a quagmire of negativity. Yes, she was going through a crisis that would make anyone sad, but her deep despair stemmed from her old belief systems. Belief systems evolve when we're young children and we carry them forward into our adult lives. These belief systems are like a roadmap of our life; they form all of our perceptions about the world, ourselves and other people. As the Buddha succinctly said,

"Our life is the creation of our mind."

We all have belief systems about marriage, children, work, and parents, to name a few. Some of these beliefs are conscious and some are unconscious. Some support us, and some sabotage our happiness and our relationships with others.

Commonly, with age and maturity, we reassess some of these belief systems. For example, you may have been taught in Sunday church services as a child that you should fear God. As you grew older, you may have read about other religions, studied philosophy, or met others with different belief systems and began to adjust or clarify your personal beliefs. When you're confronted with different ways of thinking, you may choose to keep some beliefs and discard others. As an adult, you gain the ability and opportunities to make a conscious choice about your beliefs.

Your mother and father grew up in a world where there were fewer choices available to people, and less emphasis on self-awareness. They may never have questioned the beliefs they held or passed on to their children.

What values and beliefs do you hold as an adult? Did you choose them consciously, or did you inherit them? Our values are developed from our belief systems. Individuals commonly value honesty, family, responsibility, health, commitment, education, and respect, to name a few. Being aware of your values and living your life from that knowledge brings integrity, happiness, and peace. Couples who have common values are more compatible and tend to have less conflict in their relationships. By coming to understand your values, beliefs, and the coping styles you've learned in order to maintain relationships, you will be able to discern which are working for you and which aren't. Then you can consciously choose to alter them.

You may have heard of the "frog story." I apologize to frog lovers at the onset. If you have a pot of lukewarm water and you put a frog into it and turn the heat on high, the frog will boil to death. If you have a pot of boiling water and you place a frog into it, the frog will quickly jump out. This frog knows instinctively that this isn't a safe environment and runs for its life! This is a good description of how we unknowingly stay stuck in milieus that are toxic or unhealthy because they're familiar. We become accustomed because of our limiting beliefs, coping styles, and intergenerational patterns.

Self-limiting belief systems often interfere with or cause pain in our relationships. Brainsense is the process of becoming consciously aware of your belief systems and coping behaviors. In this chapter, you will do a self-assessment, igniting the process of awareness. Later in this book, you'll learn creative tools that can help you combat these old thinking habits.

Self-Limiting Beliefs Can Sabotage Us

Limiting belief systems can be described as patterns of beliefs we hold about ourselves that restrict or constrain us in our lives. Everyone these days love acronyms, so let's call them LBs. Some common LBs include, "I'm a failure/not good enough," "I'm alone," "I'm unimportant/unlovable," and "I'm bad." They're distorted perceptions of ourselves. They're not reality. Dr. Jeffrey Young, psychologist and author of *Reinventing Your Life*, calls these patterns "lifetraps." He contends that we learn these beliefs in childhood and they reverberate into our adult life. These belief systems are automatically passed from generation to generation with most of us completely unaware of what's happening. Bruce Lipton, Ph.D., cell biologist and author of *The Biology of Belief,* has found evidence that these limiting beliefs are embedded on a cellular level. Moreover, many diseases are caused by the stress that these unconscious beliefs create.

When I work with families and assess their self-limiting beliefs, I find that parents and children often have similar LBs. Interestingly, it's not only within families where we see intergenerational patterns or behaviors. Organizations, cities, and towns display various cultural quirks. I experienced this several years ago on a sunny July day in the Thousand Islands. Spending time on the St. Lawrence River had become a passion for my family. There are many quaint and beautiful islands, villages, and towns along the river. One town in particular caught our eye, so we decided to boat over to see what their annual Pirates Day was all about. My husband and I were peacefully floating, waiting for the events to occur on the water, when suddenly we were inundated by boats with pirate flags, buckets, and water pistols. Two huge pirate ships plowed through the center of the channel and other boats were furiously chasing one another, spraying their water guns, throwing buckets of water and yelling "Arrrrr, matey." People of all ages were crazily laughing, refilling their pistols and buckets as fast as you could say Jiminy Cricket. Meanwhile, cannons were blasting in the background and the two pirate ships were steaming toward us. What a zoo! To us, it looked like total chaos, a disaster waiting to happen; however, to these boaters and villagers, it was a blast. This was an annual celebration of their history, passed down from generation to generation.

After we escaped from the pirates I realized that my reaction to this "silly behaviour" was partially coming from **my** limiting beliefs. I wasn't able to get into the spirit of Pirate Days because my old rules - you don't let go and have fun nor do you draw attention to yourself with such silliness, were propelling my discomfort. I was also absorbing my husbands' anxiety. Having this conscious awareness allowed me to have a ball the following summer in this quaint little town.

Pioneering psychologist Alfred Adler and many other therapists today believe that we develop our perceptions of ourselves, other people, and the world between the ages of 0 to 7. In these early years, we watch those around us, and interpret and misinterpret life events, all the while creating our belief systems. Adler says this results in what he calls our "private logic." It's so private we don't even know what it is! Then, as adults, we subconsciously make choices from these distorted belief systems. As a young child, we didn't have the brain capacity to be aware of our patterns and the belief systems underneath them. We just did what we knew. Now as adults, we have this capacity and can make conscious choices to shift or adjust these belief systems.

As children, our brains are not wired to understand different perspectives on life situations, consequently leading us to see it through only one lens. For example, if our teacher or parent was having a bad day, we often believed we were the cause of their foul mood. Because of our egocentric nature in that developmental period of our lives, we believed that we had caused or created others' anger or sadness. We saw the world in relation only to ourselves, and were unable to separate ourselves from others. Consequently, we came to believe that we're responsible for others' feelings and they in return are responsible for ours. From these misinterpretations, we then began to develop our self-limiting beliefs about ourselves.

As adults, our limiting beliefs (LBs) are not always triggered by intense events, but can be activated or triggered by minor circumstances such as our partner being annoyed at us, our children ignoring us, or a friend being late for a lunch date. Most of us are not aware of what's happening. We just feel angry, irritated, rejected, or sad. And the other people we're interacting with certainly don't have a clue about what's going on, especially if they get an earful! Basically, our unconscious minds continually replay negative memories, influencing our present day thoughts, feelings and behaviors.

Imagine a sandbox. If you were to take half a cup of sand in your hands, that would represent your conscious mind. The remainder of the sand is your unconscious mind, and it has immense power over your life until you cultivate your awareness. You can't do anything about patterns you don't even know are there!

The Past Can Become the Present

Our mothers grew up in a time when change didn't occur as rapidly as it does today. They didn't necessarily think about whether the old way of doing things still worked for them or was the best way of operating. There was nothing to alert them to the fact that they had other choices that might suit them better.

Today, it's clear that when we ignore the reality that our relationships and our lives aren't what we want them to be, we are unhappy. We look around us and see people who made different choices or who have different ways of communicating and relating to others than our own, and we question our beliefs and habits. Are we stuck in the past, responding to life as our mothers did, without considering that there might be a different way?

The past becomes the present when our beliefs are rooted in conditions that no longer exist. Carolyn Litty tells a story that illustrates this phenomenon well. Two fish, a barracuda and a mackerel, were placed in an aquarium and separated by a glass partition. The barracuda saw the mackerel and charged toward the glass, bumping up against it. Again and again, it swam forward, stopped each time by the barrier. When the glass partition was then removed, a most peculiar thing happened. The barracuda charged towards the mackerel and stopped at the exact same spot where the glass partition had been. We are very much like the barracuda once the partition is removed— held back by our perceptions of the world, even though they have no substance and are imaginary.

Sometimes, our self-limiting beliefs were created based on false interpretations of events, like the barracuda. In our innocence, we reasoned that if Mother was angry, it was our fault, or if Father scolded us, it was because we were bad or inadequate (you'll learn more about why we create these false impressions later in this book).

When we hold on to our LBs (limiting beliefs) or are emotionally triggered by them, we are likely to overreact to circumstances. How often do you become reactive even though you promised yourself that you would stay calm and communicate with reason? Unfortunately, our distorted stories and LBs have a huge impact on our lives and relationships.

Remember, you don't have to believe everything your mind says. To help dismantle my negative belief system, I remind myself daily of this.

A Window Into Me

Below you will find a self-assessment of your limiting belief systems. I encourage you to be honest in completing your questions. There are no right or wrong answers. This important information will be used throughout the book.

Limiting Beliefs Questionnaire

Read each question and answer it using the following scale:

0 - Not at all

1 - Sometimes

2 - Often

3 - Most of the time

_____   Do you avoid conflict?

_____   Are you a people pleaser who seeks approval?

_____   Do you fear rejection?

_____   When you are upset, do you feel that you're not important?

_____   Are you accommodating with others?

_____   Do you feel guilty or selfish if you put yourself first?

Total L _____

____ Are you defensive when criticized?

____ Are you critical of yourself and others?

____ Is your sense of self often built on your successes?

____ Do you gravitate toward critical partners?

____ Are you fearful of your faults being exposed?

____ When you are upset, do you feel that you are defective?

Total D _____

____ Do you feel like an outsider in life?

____ Do you feel lonely?

____ Do you feel that you are different?

____ Are you self-conscious about your physical appearance?

____ Were you teased or rejected as a child?

____ As a child, did you develop solitary activities because you did not feel that you belonged?

Total A _____

_____ Do you feel like a failure compared to others?

_____ Do you tend to procrastinate?

_____ Do you focus on the negative and minimize the positives?

_____ Are you working below your potential?

_____ When you are upset, do you feel you are stupid and untalented?

_____ Were your parents (or was your parent) critical?

Total F _____

Grand Total (L, D, A, F) _____

If your grand total is 40 or higher, your limiting beliefs are most likely ruling your life. You may have frequent episodes of anxiety, sadness, or depression. The higher your score, the more your limiting beliefs are holding you back from creating the relationships and the life you desire. If you scored between 30 and 40, it may indicate that you can be reactive in life situations and may have a fragile sense of self. If your total is under 25, you probably have a good grasp on your limiting beliefs, and a healthy self-esteem.

If your highest score was in the L section, your limiting belief is probably **"I'm not lovable/ important/worthy."**

If your highest score was in the D section, your limiting belief is probably **"I'm defective/bad."**

If your highest score was in the A section, your limiting belief is probably **"I'm alone."**

If your highest score was in the F section, your limiting belief is probably **"I'm a failure/not good enough."**

Four Common Stories We Make Up

In my years as a psychotherapist, and from other therapists' research, I've discovered that an individual's LBs (limiting beliefs) can be categorized into four misperceptions: being unlovable/unimportant; being defective/bad; being alone, and feeling like a failure or not good enough.

Defectiveness

As children, we may have perceived and misinterpreted the behaviors of our parents and the people close to us and subconsciously came to the conclusion that we're bad or defective. For example, after a long day at work, our parents may have been tired and irritable with us. We had no way of knowing why Mom or Dad was angry and might have assumed that we were somehow the cause of our parents' behavior or were somehow a disappointment to them. Some children hear their frustrated parents make comments such as "You're a bad boy" or "I don't know why I even had you." When these words and/or physical punishment are inflicted upon children, they often end up feeling shame, which leads to the perception that they're defective.

Unlovable/Unimportant

The belief that we're unlovable, unimportant, or unworthy are other distortions we create about ourselves as young children. Children whose parents were not able to provide support and love because of their own life situations or pain may come to believe themselves to be undeserving of love. Some parents have financial or marital problems that cause them to be depressed, angry, or distracted. Consequently, the children may experience an absence of attention, affection, understanding, or guidance.

I'm a Failure/Not Good enough

The belief that you've failed, will fail, or are inadequate compared to others is another common limiting belief. Children, who are told that they're stupid or inept, or who are frequently judged and criticized, may develop this self-limiting belief about themselves. If children's gifts and strengths are undervalued or ignored, they often end up feeling as though they've failed their parents. For example, a child may love playing the piano, however if his/her parents place more emphasis on sports, the child may suppress their talents in order to conform. At the other end of the spectrum, children of parents with perfectionistic tendencies and high expectations of themselves and others may feel that they're never good enough, no matter what they do. This may also lead to children comparing themselves to their peers and not measuring up, whether in school, sports, or appearance.

Alone

People who hold this limiting belief often feel that they're completely alone in life, different from other people or on the outside of life looking in. As children they may have been bullied, teased, or socially isolated, resulting in difficulties making and maintaining friendships. Additionally, some may have had feelings of being alone because their family frequently moved, their parents were socially isolated themselves or not actively involved in their children's lives, leaving the children to figure out problems or life situations on their own.

To assist you in understanding how our self-limiting beliefs can be triggered, I'll share a personal example. When I was a young teenager, I used to get annoyed when my father rearranged the dishes in the dishwasher after I had placed my plate and glass inside. Sometimes, he would not say anything to me and other times, he would say, "Put the plates beside the other plates, please." Thoughts raced through my mind, such as, "I can never do it right or good enough for him." I was seeing this situation through my limiting belief of being a failure or not good enough. My dad obviously didn't see me as a failure and his intent was to teach me. Nonetheless, I stored this memory with my other negative memories and misinterpreted the situation. Being a typical teenager, I stomped out of the kitchen leaving my father bewildered, asking, "What just happened?"

Collette's story is a great example of how our LBs trigger and/or influence our choices, behaviors and emotions in the grand scheme of life. She was raised by an aloof, critical father who didn't have time for his children. His work and Sunday football games seemed to be his focus. Collette tried all sorts of ways to get his attention and love. Needless to say, her repeated attempts failed. Unknowingly, as a teenager and adult, she gravitated towards men similar to her father. As a result, she exhausted herself trying to get them to treat her with love and spend time with her, hoping to banish her limiting belief of being unimportant or lovable. Unfortunately, Collette received the same treatment from her boyfriends that her father had given her, which further reinforced her self-limiting beliefs, spiralling her into a severe depression.

Discovering the Limiting Beliefs You Hold

Think of a recent time when you were frustrated, angry, or anxious. Record it without judgment of yourself or others; just be honest, even if you feel childish or petty.

Close your eyes and reconnect to those feelings now.

Now drift back in time, perhaps when you were a young child, and let any memories come forward. Describe these memories.

Notice how the present and past feelings are similar. Which limiting belief is this present situation triggering within you?

Often, when we do this exercise, we find our present day feelings are similar to our past memory feelings. It's uncanny how we unconsciously reexperience feelings from the past. With overwhelming power, these old feelings come rushing forward and the intensity of our present day reactions seems disproportionate to the situation.

Through both my personal and professional life, I have learned that nothing will shift in our lives until we're aware of our reoccurring patterns and begin to change our behaviors. We need to take action. Change can be a frightening thing. We long to cling to the past, when our lives seemed to be working. Nonetheless, continuing to automatically cut the ends off our pot roast can be detrimental to our relationships. Mother may not have realized that she didn't have to cut off part of the roast, and she may have been satisfied to waste the ends. You, however, may want more: more fulfilling relationships, more authenticity in your life, and more of a connection to your partner. If your mother had realized she had other choices, she might well have chosen not to cut off those ends of the roast and not to interact with others in the same old way she had been taught.

Now that you're starting to become aware of your self-limiting beliefs, you need to learn about how those beliefs result in unhealthy coping styles and donning masks to play a role in the disempowering Drama Triangle (you'll learn about the Drama Triangle in the next chapter). These habitual patterns contribute to keeping you stagnant or unhappy in relationships but fortunately, once you become aware of them, you can consciously choose new thoughts and behaviors.

Here's What You Learned

- Four most common **LBs** or lies we create about ourselves: I'm unlovable/unimportant; I'm a failure/ not good enough; I'm defective; I'm alone.

- **LBs** are formed through the eyes of a child and are thus distorted stories.

- We are all in this together. Every human being has self-limiting belief systems.

- The beauty of **LBs** is that they've been learned and can therefore be "unlearned."

- **LBs** not only impact our mental health, they also affect our physical health.

CHAPTER 2:
THE MASKS WE INHERITED

"The conscious mind is the creative one, the one that conjures up positive thoughts. In contrast, the subconscious mind is a repository of stimulus-response tapes derived from instincts and learned experiences. The subconscious mind is strictly habitual."

~ Bruce Lipton, Ph.D.

To manage the feelings that evolve from our limiting belief systems as children, we also develop coping strategies: behaviors that help us feel better because they help us protect or defend ourselves. We all have an innate yearning and need to belong, which further cultivates the development of these unconscious coping skills. As children we do not have the Brainsense, the ability to be aware of our LBs and coping styles, in order to process the feelings that arise. We may lack role models who could teach us how to develop healthy strategies so we develop ineffective ones. Persistent people pleasing, perfectionism, control, avoidance, and dependence are common coping styles you may find yourself using. Other behaviors, such as substance abuse, overworking, superiority, overeating, engaging in extramarital affairs, and procrastination may temporarily help us feel better, but are little more than short-term Band-Aids.

In times of stress and especially distress, we often resort to these unproductive coping styles in an attempt to protect ourselves. It is crucial to remember that what you learned as a child is neither right nor wrong. Now, as an adult, you may want to ask yourself if these coping styles are working. Are they providing you with peace and happiness?

What's Your M.A.S.K?

Below you will find a self-assessment of your coping styles. Think of them as the masks you wear to protect yourself from emotional pain.

In each grouping, make a check mark in front of the characteristics and behaviors that apply to you.

___ Good listener

___ Loyal

___ Warm, friendly

___ Worry what others think of me

___ Avoid conflict

___ Don't always say what I want/need

TOTAL M _____

___ Difficulty saying "No"

___ Rarely criticize; deflate with criticism

___ Like to please

___ Make others feel valued

___ Sensitive

___ Long to be appreciated

___ Optimistic

__ Extremely social

__ Dislike deadlines

__ Fun-loving

__ Very popular

__ Uncomfortable

__ Need lots of stimulation

__ Easily bored

__ High energy

__ Dislike details

__ Optimistic

__ Spontaneous

__ Difficulties with remembering commitments

__ Ideas person, weak with follow-up

TOTAL A _____

__ Logical

__ Very organized

__ Like "to do" lists

__ Detailed oriented

__ Believe "work first, then fun"

__ Important to "do it right"

__ Loyal, reliable

__ Give others advice ("I know best")

__ Fear failure/avoid it at all costs

__ Do not like sudden changes

__ Think in black and white

__ Unrealistic expectations of self and others

__ Very responsible

TOTAL S _____

__ Goal oriented	__ Boss others
__ Need to feel successful, capable	__ Weak anger control
	__ Leader
__ Assertive	__ Repress feelings
__ Direct, blunt	__ Visionary
__ Enjoys challenges	__ Organized
__ Produce results	__ Competitive

TOTAL K _____

SCORING

If you had the highest score in **M**, your coping/protective style is probably **M**ime.

If you had the highest score in **A**, your coping/protective style is probably **A**ctor/**A**ctress.

If you had the highest score in **S**, your coping/protective style is probably **S**uperman/**S**uperwoman.

If you had the highest score in **K**, your coping/protective style is probably **K**ing/Queen.

Remember, these coping strategies were developed very early in life, when you had no other means of dealing with various life events and lacked Brainsense. Now you can reexamine these strategies, decide which ones are working for you, and modify them if you choose. It is common for most of us to use more than one coping style, so you may find that you have two high scores.

Mime

Mimes tend to be persistent people pleasers, so busy attending to the needs of others that they forget to take care of their own needs. Sometimes Mimes act the way they think others want them to in order to gain approval and avoid anger. The underlying need to be liked and fear of rejection is so strong that it causes many Mimes to strive to please others and to avoid conflict. With maintaining harmony and peace as their ultimate priority, they become so focused on others that they lose sight of what's best for themselves. They say "yes" far too often and thus easily feel overwhelmed, drained, and stressed. While it does feel good to be liked and viewed as a "nice" person, over time, Mimes can become bitter and resentful. They naturally begin asking themselves, "What about me?"

A common limiting belief underlying the habit of persistent people pleasing is: "I'm not lovable, important, or worthy." If you fall into this people pleasing personality style, you may have noticed that you compensate for others' failings and attempt to overdo for others to your own detriment. I suggest that you start asking yourself the following questions: "Is what I'm doing for others draining me? Am I over-giving? Is this behavior actually preventing me from achieving my goal (namely, good relationships)?" These simple questions will help you eventually develop a keen awareness of your actions—an invaluable first step toward becoming internally focused (looking inside yourself) instead of externally focused (on things over which you have no control). Additionally, you'll be more conscious of your automatic, overly accommodating behaviors. Initially, you may still give too much to others, but in time, you'll learn to balance taking care of yourself with the joy of authentically helping others.

Actor/Actress

Individuals who develop the Actor/Actress as a coping style are usually trying to escape feelings of stress and pain. They would rather keep things light, logical, and conflict-free. They may avoid their pain by numbing their feelings, even the enjoyable ones. At times, Actors/Actresses prevent themselves from feeling positive emotions because they anticipate that negative feelings will linger; they are waiting for "the other shoe to drop." They tend to stay neutral, not allowing themselves to feel joy or sorrow, anger, or laughter. It's as if Actors/Actresses seek to simply exist rather than truly live. It's as if they dwell on "Planet Existing", where people are "human doings" versus "human beings"!

Actors/Actresses can ignore their real emotions, missing countless opportunities to connect deeply with others on an intimate level, or to allow others to connect with them. Because they've been disconnected from their emotions for so long, they may avoid situations where emotions are likely to arise. They often have trouble relating with or being compassionate toward others who are in pain, and they certainly do not know how to be compassionate toward themselves. Those feelings are too overwhelming, too unpredictable.

Beneath the Actor's/Actress's numbness is an emptiness. They long for connection, but it's too painful for them to feel these feelings on a conscious level. Consequently, they remain unaware of how they're contributing to a lack of emotional intimacy in their relationships.

Many years ago, I counseled a client named David who learned at a very young age to dull his emotions. His parents were both alcoholics in constant turmoil and pain, which created a highly unstable environment for David and his siblings. As a teenager, David turned toward alcohol to eradicate his feelings. He continued to drink and abuse drugs into his adulthood, until his wife gave him an ultimatum: Stop or get out. Fortunately, David was able to discontinue his use of these substances, but not without still feeling empty inside. He became irritable, anxious, and depressed. He existed without any joy or laughter. Ultimately, his wife decided she could not handle their marriage and left. This became a catalyst for David to begin counseling and, as he described it, he "woke up." He began exercising, joined Tae Kwon Do, and educated himself about intimate relationships and old coping styles. He moved from being an Actor into living with vitality, happiness, and peace. Moreover, David broke the intergenerational cycle of substance abuse.

Superman/Superwoman

People who develop the Superman/Superwoman coping style usually have a strong need for order in their lives. They may think that they're superior to others or simply come across that way. It's often not their intention to behave this way, but their unconscious insecurities about being a failure cultivate this behavior. Because they want everything to be done "right," they are often perfectionistic and may act as if they know best. Procrastination often goes hand in hand with perfectionism. These individuals may avoid starting a task because they want it to be perfect. Their inner self critic constantly worries about making mistakes should they allow their guard down. They're often extremely self-critical of themselves and others.

Sarah was a financial advisor who thoroughly enjoyed her job. She was detail-oriented, efficient, methodical, and serious. If Sarah made a mistake, she would attempt to find someone else to blame and would often secretively berate herself. She had several short-term relationships, but never could find anyone who was able to meet her high standards. She realized that she was pushing men away because of her critical behaviors, yet she couldn't seem to stop. Her mask was firmly in place, and it took time and patience to peel it off. Eventually, Sarah was able to see the underlying self-limiting belief that she was a failure, and how this belief was impacting her intimate relationships. It was a difficult admission, particularly as she came across as a very confident woman. However, once she accepted her LB and coping style, Sarah was able to pave a new road for herself, one open to new possibilities.

King/Queen

People with this mask or coping style tend to have a need for control. Individuals who use control as a coping strategy often express that they felt out of control as a child and don't feel a sense of control over their lives as an adult when under stress either. They avoid criticism and when faced with it, often have an intense emotional reaction. Typically, Kings and Queens have difficulty admitting that they use control as a coping strategy in their lives, as this might mean that they're doing something "wrong." Perceiving that they're in control reassures Kings and Queens that they're "important." With this coping style comes a need to not only control their own feelings and behaviors, but those of others as well. However, these behaviors often backfire as people often don't want to be controlled and become critical and resentful. Unfortunately, they set themselves up for what they're trying to avoid.

I had a client named Debra, who as a child, often felt that events were completely out of her control. Her father was physically and emotionally abusive to her mother. Debra would try to protect her mother; she would lay awake many nights listening to see if her mother was okay and became hypervigilant, constantly observing her parents. At night, Debra would get out of bed to ask her parents for a glass of water so that she'd get their attention and perhaps stop the abuse. To cope with the horrible feelings of anxiety this situation provoked, she started to believe that if she kept alert and watchful, she might be able to prevent or rescue her mother from the abuse. Because her parents were reacting out of their own self-limiting beliefs, they were unable to be nurturing, supportive parents to Debra. Like other young children in this type of situation, Debra interpreted her parents' neglect as evidence that she was "bad."

As children, we cannot understand that we have absolutely no ability to change an abusive relationship or stop adults from behaving abusively toward each other. A young brain does not yet have the capacity to logically think through situations and see the limits of our ability to influence them. Debra resorted to trying to control her surroundings and focused on keeping her room extremely neat and tidy. Her hope was that this would make her father happy and then he would no longer hurt her mother. Subconsciously, she was trying to control her father's feelings in order to protect her mother, believing that if she succeeded, perhaps her own needs for love and attention could be met. How tightly we cling to these masks! Even when we're presented with plenty of evidence that our self-limiting beliefs are distorted, we often don't let go of the mask we inherited.

As a teenage girl, I was mesmerised by the gorgeous movie stars Raquel Welch and Elizabeth Taylor. I had never heard of Marilyn Monroe until I was in my teens and saw a picture of this beautiful woman. I had vaguely heard of her and was totally confused about why such an attractive woman would end her life. Then I heard Elton John's ode to Marilyn, using her real name, "Good-bye, Norma Jean." I listened intently to his lyrics about being a candle in the wind, and not knowing who to turn to when the rain sets in. Whether she called herself Norma Jean or Marilyn Monroe didn't seem to matter. The result was the same: She didn't have a true sense of who she was and craved external approval that could never make up for the emptiness she felt inside. We've seen this repeated on the world stage in the lives and deaths of celebrities who resort to using external substances to medicate their emotional pain, and in so doing die a tragic death.

As a psychotherapist, I can understand how self-limiting beliefs and coping strategies contribute to a person's demise. In Marilyn's case, she was raised in and out of foster homes and never gained a true sense of her inner beauty and innate strengths. I would venture to guess that her limiting belief was that she was unlovable or unimportant, and she coped with these tormenting feelings by focusing on pleasing others and thereby hoping to gain external approval and admiration.

Some people decide to explore their self-limiting beliefs and intergenerational beliefs once stress, depression, or anxiety enters their life. Often, it's precipitated by a loss of some kind, either through a breakup or the loss of a loved one. It's human nature for us to go about our lives in the status quo, oblivious to old patterns. We don't often see the need to become self-reflective until we hit a bump in the road called life, or a "flat tire" that stops us from functioning. In my work, I see the great benefit in exploring old patterns *before* a crisis occurs, as a preventative measure. Even if you aren't experiencing great suffering as a result of your mask, I hope you will take up the challenge of being proactive and letting go of your self-limiting behaviors and your mask. With this new awareness, you may also be able to recognize your partners, friends or family members' masks and realize that they are probably being triggered by their own LBs. This awareness can sometimes assist you in not personalizing others behaviors. In the next chapter you will learn tools and techniques to shift negative habits and alter how you communicate. First, however, you need to know the healthy coping strategies that will help you stick to your commitment to let go of your self-limiting beliefs.

A Healthy Balance of Coping Techniques

Certainly, our mothers believed in a healthy, balanced meal. They learned from their own mothers the importance of balancing meat, vegetables, fruits, dairy, breads, fats, and sweets. What they didn't know is that balance is just as important when it comes to the coping techniques we use to manage stress.

As previously mentioned, our limiting beliefs and intergenerational patterns sometimes prevent us from developing healthy coping styles as young children. As we mature, most individuals cultivate more effective coping strategies. There are many healthy coping strategies—self-awareness, trusting your intuition, problem solving, and exercising, to name a few. Dr. Schwarzer, a psychologist, observed that as long as individuals believe they can handle issues in their lives and are optimistic, they more effectively deal with life events. The six coping strategies he has identified are:

Proactive Coping

Reflective Coping

Strategic Planning

Preventative Coping

Instrumental Support Seeking

Emotional Support Seeking

Each of these strategies is useful, and ideally, you would use more than one, balancing your "diet" of techniques. Problems arise when you stick with just one and start to develop a pattern of behavior that causes difficulties in your relationships. Let's look at the six healthy coping strategies one by one.

Proactive Coping

Individuals who engage in Proactive Coping tend to have a "take charge" personality, enjoy challenges, set goals for themselves, and aim to attain those goals. They're effective problem solvers, they jump right into the muck, always finding a way to work around any roadblocks or detours life presents. Learning from trial and error is par for the course.

Reflective Coping

People who use Reflective Coping methodically think internally about how to tackle a situation and often imagine different scenarios in their minds.

They're not impulsive in their coping style, and may want to know the best answer before moving to problem solving.

Strategic Planning

List making, breaking down problems into manageable parts, and focusing on the most important part first are all ways that strategic individuals deal with life. They, too, are very task and goal-oriented.

Preventative Coping

"Be prepared," or "It's better to be forewarned and forearmed," are the likely mottos of people with this coping style. They think, act, and plan ahead to avoid possible disasters. Unexpected circumstances can create imbalance and stress in their lives.

Instrumental Support Seeking

When under stress, these individuals are quick to seek advice from others. Discussing issues with friends helps them see different perspectives and feel increased confidence in their decisions.

Emotional Support Seeking

Individuals with this coping style rely on others to help them feel better or deal with problems. They share their feelings freely and seek empathy from their family, friends, and coworkers.

Again, each of these coping strategies can be healthy if used in moderation and in balance with each other. For example, individuals who use Proactive Coping are likely to attain their goals, but they can become so focused and driven that they steamroll over others. Individuals who seek emotional support from friends and family can become too dependent and can feel helpless and incapable of dealing with situations when no one else is around. Learning to combine these different coping strategies creates the balance we all need.

Another coping mechanism that has been researched by psychologists for years is called "blowing off steam," or venting. Some researchers do not believe it's a healthy way of coping while others do. Psychologist James Pennebaker, Ph.D., found in his research that people who vented or got things off their chests were healthier. However, he stresses that blowing off steam isn't as important as making sense of situations, feelings, or events. In his book, *Opening Up: The Healing Power of Expressing Emotions,* Dr. Pennebaker suggests that you write all of your thoughts and emotions on paper without censoring them. After a few days, he says, most of us will re-evaluate the situation and perhaps have new insights after we've calmed down. To help you make sense of situations, he suggests you ask yourself two questions: "Why did this happen?" and "What good might I derive from it?" People who do not make sense of circumstances or emotions can get caught in ruminating and obsessing, which creates stress and distress.

Recording your feelings and thoughts on paper will also allow you to more clearly see your limiting beliefs. I also suggest recording your behaviors or reactions in order to identify effective and ineffective coping styles. Themes and patterns are easier to observe when in black and white. I understand that it may be difficult to record your feelings, but it's a tactic that provides opportunities for personal growth and relief from stress, so I highly recommend the practice!

Jeff and Donna's Masks: An Example of How Limiting Beliefs and Imbalanced Coping Styles Harm Our Relationships

In your relationships with your partner, children, and family, old programs often get triggered or activated without your awareness. A simple situation can get blown out of proportion leading to anger, withdrawal, and unnecessary hurt. Then you go into protection mode, trying not to feel the pain of your limiting beliefs.

Many years ago, I counseled a couple who were trying to figure out whether to go their separate ways and divorce or stay married. Donna complained about taking second place to all of her husband's activities. Work, golf, friends, and sports always seemed to be his priorities. Jeff felt nagged and smothered and didn't want to come home from work at the end of the day. As time went on, they both began to withdraw from each other, feeling angry, resentful, and lonely. When I met them in my office, they were both feeling discouraged and helpless.

One of the first things we looked at were their self-limiting beliefs about themselves. As a child, Donna's perception had been that if she was good girl, did not make any waves, performed well in school and pleased her parents, they would, in return, make her feel special and important. People pleasing (the Mime) became her way of coping and it created a false sense of belonging. Her self-limiting belief was that she was unimportant/unlovable. Consequently, she feared rejection and anger as that confirmed her unconscious view of herself. She lost touch with what she liked and what her opinions were, as well as her goals, talents, and strengths.

As a young boy, Jeff perceived that he couldn't do anything right, and would never be able to live up to his parents' standards and expectations. He believed that if he strived to work harder and harder at every-thing he touched, he could fulfill their expectations. Consequently, he excelled academically and was a top athlete. Jeff's limiting belief about himself was that he was a failure/not good enough. Even when his performance was outstanding, he would raise the bar even more, not knowing how to celebrate his accomplishments. If someone gave him constructive advice, Jeff would interpret it as an indication that he wasn't good enough. Then he would get angry, withdraw, or relentlessly chastise himself. On the M.A.S.K questionnaire, Jeff scored high in the "Superman" category, with a need for order and to be superior.

When Donna and Jeff married, their old subconscious patterns and scripts about how they should be as a wife and husband kicked in. For example, one of Donna's subconscious scripts was to put her partner first at all times. She had grown up in a household where her mother displayed this behavior, so Donna automatically, unknowingly did the same. She realized that balancing self and others is important for a healthy relationship, yet she continued this behavior pattern. On the other hand, Jeff's subconscious belief about husbands was that they should have the final say on decisions.

With time, most of our old scripts become irritating. Eventually, Donna became tired of pleasing Jeff, keeping the peace, and not getting anything in return. Her limiting belief that she was unimportant triggered her emotions, which caused her to explode or implode and to get easily angered or depressed. Meanwhile, Jeff was trying to convince himself and others that he was "good enough" by working 24/7. He interpreted Donna's pleas for spending more time together as evidence that he was not doing it right and not being a good husband. Consequently, he would stay away from home to avoid these uncomfortable feelings. It was clear that their negative inner states were sabotaging their marriage, as they were stuck in old belief systems and coping strategies.

Both Jeff and Donna knew intellectually that they were lovable, confident individuals; that's what their logical minds told them. However, emotionally, they still held on to old beliefs and triggered each other. It's almost as if we shrink into our little kid selves when our old patterns are activated, unknowingly reliving the pain of past experiences.

With awareness and acceptance of their self-limiting beliefs and ineffective coping styles, Donna and Jeff were able to recognize when their old patterns were getting activated and inform each other that they were triggered. They would then take a break from their discussions in order to calm down, allowing them to deal with their issues in mature, empathetic ways. Ultimately, they learned to communicate differently with each other. Their respect and love toward each other was reignited and they remained together.

The Drama Triangle: Victim, Rescuer, Persecutor

Stephen Karpman, M.D., came up with an effective tool for helping people increase their awareness of their unconscious coping styles. His Drama Triangle describes how we get into the "blame game" in our relationships and fail to be accountable for our behavior, becoming defensive in a lose-lose paradigm.

There are three roles in this Drama Triangle—that of the victim, rescuer, and persecutor. We learn these roles as powerless young children, and often continue playing these roles into adulthood. Let's look at them individually:

People who take on the role of **victim** often perceive that they can't handle life or take care of themselves. They hold the unconscious belief that they always need someone stronger than they are because they feel alone, they're weak and incompetent. With these limiting beliefs, self-proclaimed victims can become dependent on their primary relationships. At times, victims cannot see their talents, nor do they set goals or strive to live life to the fullest because they see themselves as incapable of success. Thoughts such as "Oh, I could never do that" or "That's for other smarter people" rattle on relentlessly. Their minds become prison cells.

Rescuers, however, often have a limiting belief that their needs are not important or that they're not as worthy as others. To compensate for this, they like to take care of others and become "fixers." This helps them feel important and needed. Underlying their need to fix others is also the unconscious belief that "If I take care of others, eventually they will take care of me." This rarely happens because they often choose victims to dote on who do not have the capacity to take care of others. A person can't be a rescuer without a victim to "rescue." People playing the victim and rescuer roles unconsciously gravitate towards each other due to self-limiting beliefs and old coping strategies. For example, a person who uses people pleasing as a coping style will often connect with a partner who uses control. It appears to be a perfect match. The people pleaser doesn't like making decisions and their partners do. The people pleaser doesn't like conflict, so they don't challenge their partners.

This arrangement suits the person who likes to be in control as well as the people pleaser—for a while. With time, however, the pleaser may become angry and resentful of being told what to do, and withdraw or become passive aggressive. The controlling person usually doesn't understand or like this behavior change, and may become even more controlling.

Persecutors often have deep-seated feelings of low self-worth and the subconscious belief that they are bad. To avoid feeling vulnerable, they develop a coping style of dominating others through bullying, aggression, and lecturing. They often project their negative feelings about themselves onto others, as it is too painful to acknowledge these feelings within themselves. An example of projection would be accusing others of being bossy and aggressive when, in fact, they are displaying these behaviors themselves.

Persecutors become isolated because their temperament is so brash. Like rescuers, they, too, need a victim, someone to blame so that they can avoid owning their behaviors in various situations.

Interestingly, when on the Drama Triangle, we can play any of the three roles. For example, if the victim gets tired of being taken care of, he or she can slide into the persecutor role and become quite angry and resentful towards the rescuer. Likewise, if the rescuer begins to resent always being the caretaker, he or she can become a persecutor as well. I've witnessed clients playing out the victim, rescuer, and persecutor with themselves. One minute they're acting like a victim and then they jump into the persecutor role, beating themselves up with a verbal barrage for feeling that way.

To get out of the Drama Triangle, we first need to be aware that we're in it. We fall into the familiar patterns of blaming others and berating ourselves. Being accountable for our part of the Drama Triangle is a key step in breaking free of this dynamic. One way to figure out if you're on the Drama Triangle is to notice your negative thoughts. Are you pointing the finger at others? If so, do a 180 degree shift and look at yourself in a nonjudgmental way. Jim Collins, author of *Good to Great: Why Some Companies Make the Leap and Other's Don't,* uses a metaphor of the window and the mirror. He suggests we stop looking out the window and start looking in the mirror at ourselves. When you turn your eyes toward yourself, do so with curiosity. Ask yourself what role you've fallen into – victim, rescuer, persecutor. Ask, "What's going on inside me? Am I feeling helpless and incapable or angry because things are not going my way?"

The Real You and Me: The Johari Window

You may be wondering why more people aren't self-aware? There are many answers to this question. One is by using the Johari Window, which explains the process of human interactions. It was developed by Joseph Luft and Harry Ingham in 1955 as a way to understand communication and relationships. As you come to understand it, you'll see that the more the real, authentic "you" is hidden from others and yourself, the more difficult it can be to sustain loving relationships.

∞

I. KNOWN TO SELF AND OTHERS	II. KNOWN TO OTHERS AND NOT SELF
III. KNOWN TO SELF AND NOT KNOWN TO OTHERS	IV. NOT KNOWN TO SELF OR OTHERS

In this diagram, you'll see the four quadrants Joe and Harry (Johari!) developed. The first quadrant refers to information known to yourself and to others. This includes factual information like your name and phone number, and can extend to more personal information such as feelings, desires, and intentions. It's information that both self and others are consciously aware of.

The second quadrant speaks of information others perceive about you that you are *not* aware of. It could be something minor, like the chocolate on your face from lunchtime, to something more interpersonal like how you're not a good listener. In this case, you are not conscious of what others easily see in you.

The third quadrant refers to knowledge known to you and not to others. As you develop relationships with people and trust them, you may share more about yourself and thus expand this window. For example, you may initially share your favorite movies and books with someone, and then when you're more comfortable, you further expand this quadrant by disclosing your mistakes in life or your deepest fears.

The fourth quadrant denotes information not known to self or others. This quadrant refers to knowledge we store in our unconsciousness, such as our self-limiting beliefs or intergenerational patterns previously described. It can also refer to knowledge we don't yet have. Attending a workshop or course can open the doors to expanded information to self and others. Novel experiences and events can bring fresh insights and expand this quadrant. I hope this book is sparking new insights and opening up this quadrant for you.

Awareness of quadrant II, III, and IV can assist you in figuring out your emotional triggers. As you become more cognizant of your LBs, your self-awareness expands. The more aware you are, the more you can choose to learn, grow, or do things differently, potentially increasing your levels of self-confidence. Moreover, this may also propel you to ask others you trust to lovingly share with you their perceptions of you, perhaps revealing your blind spots (quadrant II). This takes courage. It's not easy to see or admit to our limitations. However, knowing and accepting ourselves, warts and all, is part of our human evolution and can bring tremendous joy and peace within ourselves and towards others. The more we accept ourselves—the "real" us, not the selves we are when we wear masks or play a role in the drama triangle—the more we can discern what is best for ourselves. With acceptance and awareness, we can create mature relationships and engage each other from a place of confidence and nurturance.

Behaviors and Emotions That Stem from Limiting Beliefs

The following is a list of coping behaviors and emotions that can be rooted in your LBs. You may find that you exhibit some of these traits but not others. It may be painful to consider that you engage in these behaviors. However, the more cognizant you are of these actions, the easier they are to control. Moreover, these feelings and behaviors can be cues or reminders that your LBs are activated and controlling your life.

Self-centeredness	People pleasing	Self-hatred
Resentful	Self-reliant	Superiority
Angry	Lusting	Resistance to growth
Jealous	Defiant	Self-pitying
Rationalizing	Shouting	Intimidating
Critical	Justifying	Impulsive
Self-pitying	Argumentative	Perfectionist
Suspicious	Judgmental	Narrow-minded

Controlling	Hypersensitive	Blocking
Overly emotional	Narrow-minded	Compulsive
Worrying	Inconsiderate	Denying
Withdrawn	Forgetful	Attacking
Domineering	Fantasizing	Apathetic
Self-righteous	Self-destructive	Competitive
Intolerant	Ungrateful	Boastful
Gossiping	Fearful	Impatient
Apprehensive	Sullen	Willful
Deceitful	Rescuer	Procrastination
Dishonest	Violent	Discouraging
Indifferent	Careless	Secretive
Depressed	Projecting	Pessimistic
Obscene	Dependent	Aggression
Lying	Arrogance	Demanding
Contradictory	Paranoid	Complying
Spiteful	Negative	Distracted
Irresponsible	Nagging	Dramatizing
Overly optimistic	Indulgent	Cowardice
Whining	Avoidance	Blaming
Vindictive	Insecure	Greed
Victim	Enabling	
Rebellious	Undisciplined	

∞

I hope that after reading the first two chapters you realize that many of the problems you've faced in your life have stemmed from old patterns, and that the real you can express itself when you let go of the masks and roles that have held you back. Gradually you begin to use coping techniques more effectively - you don't have to automatically do what you were taught long ago. You can choose new behaviors and beliefs that your mother may not have known about, as you'll see.

Here Is What You Learned

- You learned at a young age to cope by being a Mime, Actor/Actress, Superman/Superwoman, and/or King/Queen. These coping styles may not be working for you now.

- There are several coping techniques which, when balanced, are healthy for you.

- You develop your coping styles unconsciously as a protective mechanism. You have a choice to let them go if you choose.

- Your LBs and unhealthy or imbalanced coping styles create stress, depression, and anxiety.

- The Johari Window reveals that how you perceive yourself may be different from how others perceive you. Knowing what you are willing to share with others and willing to have them share with you will help you become self-aware and let go of old coping styles that aren't working for you.

CHAPTER 3:
THE BEST ADVICE
YOUR MOTHER
WOULD GIVE
YOU NOW

*"First I was dying to finish high school
and start college.*

*And then I was dying to finish college
and start working.*

*And then I was dying to marry
and have children.*

*And then I was dying for my children
to grow old enough
for school so I could return to work.*

And then I was dying to retire.

*And now, I am dying... and suddenly
I realize I forgot to live."*

Anonymous

Our mothers gave us the best advice they could, but if they knew what's in this chapter, they could have spared themselves and us many hard earned life lessons. Among the advice they would have given us is:

- *Change Your Brain*
- *Practice Acceptance and Self-Compassion*
- *Embrace the Three C's: Feeling Connected, Capable, and Counted*
- *Lighten Up!*
- *Live By the Five Brainsense Principles*

Change Your Brain

To change your brain, you have to understand some basics about how it works when it perceives danger. We take in information from our surroundings through our five senses—smell, sight, taste, touch, and sound. This information travels into our brains through our feeling center, called the limbic system. The limbic system controls the old survival, fight-or-flight mechanism inherited from our ancestors. If the limbic system perceives something to be dangerous it automatically responds with either fight or flight. Every threatening memory we store can activate the limbic system's response. After the information goes through the limbic system, it travels to the area of the brain called the frontal cortex, where we can think with logic and reason.

Our LBs trigger our fight-or-flight process, intensifying our feelings, preventing our emotions and logic from working together. We get stuck because our strong, negative memories and emotions, generated by the limbic system, dominate our thinking. We know how we want to behave, but we initially feel we can't. **Brainsense** is the process of becoming aware of your LBs and Masks, knowing when they're triggered, and creating different methods of coping and behaving. Developing **Brainsense** allows the interaction and balance between our emotions and logic to strengthen, and then we're more in control of our thoughts and feelings. We actually retrain and rewire our brains, decrease the response of the limbic system, and not allow our old patterns to dominate. We'll stop overreacting to situations that aren't truly dangerous and instead, respond to them with clarity and calmness.

Jonathan Haidt, in his book *The Happiness Hypothesis*, describes this interaction between logic and emotion with the analogy of a rider on an elephant. The rider is the logic and reason; it is conscious. The elephant is the emotion, gut feelings, knee-jerk reaction and intuition; it is unconscious. Haidt states that ultimately, the elephant has the most power. For the rider and the elephant to work together, we must take time to be aware of the elephant or the unconscious patterns.

New brain research has discovered that our brains are highly malleable. We can actually change our brains! Psychologist Donald Hebb realised in 1949 that "when neurons fire together, they wire together." Our thoughts actually create neuropathways in our brains. Many recent researchers have concurred with Dr. Hebb including Daniel Siegal, author of

The Developing Mind, and Rick Hanson, author of *Buddha's Brain: The Practical Neuroscience of Happiness, Love and Wisdom.* Dr. Hanson encourages individuals to incorporate new positive actions daily, which then cumulatively creates larger changes in both our behaviors, and in our brains. This new research is profound as it supports the fact that we have the ability to shift our LBs by reorganizing our thoughts, producing new neural pathways.

Why is it so important to change our brains? First, of course, it will lead to greater satisfaction in our relationships and everyday life, because we'll find it easier to make healthy choices about our beliefs and behaviors. There's another reason to reprogram our brains, however: The mind-body connection ensures that healthier thoughts and behaviors foster better physical health which in turn fosters healthier thoughts and behaviors.

When you're young, you go to bed every night expecting to wake up every morning. And as you go through your days, you also expect that you will nestle into your bed again every evening. It's not uncommon to be so focused on your external world that you're oblivious to your body, unaware of what goes on under your skin that keeps you healthy and functioning. How often do you think about the heart pumping blood into every vein in your body or about the red blood cells that transport oxygen? When you do stop to think about your body and perhaps remember some of your biology lessons from high school, you may be astounded at your complex internal systems. I marvel at how everything runs automatically: how our fingers know how to move and our legs know when to walk.

The mind and the body work together efficiently. From a health perspective, continual emotional overreactions or suppression of emotions can create illness and disease. When our limbic system perceives a threat, whether or not that threat is real, our brains release hormones that initiate the fight-or-flight response of quick energy, shallow breathing, and rapid heart rate. Unfortunately, our negative beliefs can fool our brains into thinking there's a real threat, and these stress hormones are emitted unnecessarily. If these hormones are released too often, over the course of years they can contribute to many illnesses. Emotional stress caused by the perception of danger or threat actually compromises our health.

Stress, anxiety, depression, and disease can evolve from our limiting beliefs, which create mental chatter, negative self-talk that constantly replays in our mind. In 1995, stress was an associated risk factor in three of the top ten causes of death in Americans: heart disease, suicide, and strokes.

Over the decades, researchers have discovered that stress is also linked to cancer. Linda Temoshok, psychologist at the University of California, and her colleagues coined a specific personality style, "Type

C personality," which seems to be more susceptible to cancer. These individuals tend to overinvest themselves emotionally in specific parts of their lives—marriage, children, or career—in order to feel important or lovable. Unfortunately, if one of these aspects of his or her life is threatened by loss, such as an impending divorce or their children reaching the age where they're going to leave home and start college, the person with Type C personality is flooded with feelings of helplessness, despair, and rejection, similar to what was experienced in childhood. This continual feeling of helplessness spurs the brain to emit excessive amounts of unhealthy chemicals into our bodies. This is what researchers believe contributes to the development of cancer. Remembering the mind-body connection can help you stay emotionally stable and physically healthy by shifting your LBs and old coping strategies.

As Mohandas Gandhi said so eloquently:

"Your beliefs become your thoughts
Your thoughts become your words
Your words become your actions
Your actions become your habits
Your habits become your values
Your values become your destiny."

Practice Acceptance and Self-Compassion

Learning to look at ourselves with curiosity and acceptance rather than judgment and distaste allows self-awareness to evolve. Acceptance allows forward movement. Acceptance empowers us to take back control of our minds, behaviors, brains, and health. Without awareness and acceptance, we continue to live from false stories (self-limiting beliefs) or, as some psychotherapists call it, our "false self." When we function from our false self, we are never truly happy or satisfied. We are dependent on external factors such as approval, money, people/relationships, substances, or work. But external factors are inconsistent; we may lose our jobs, investments, or relationships, leaving us feeling empty.

One of my all time favorite authors, Elizabeth Kubler-Ross states,

*"Our real power is not derived from our positions in life, a hefty bank account or an impressive career... it is the expression of that **authenticity** inside of us. Our power lies deep within us."*

Unfortunately, society promotes power in our work, relationships, and with our children. Being our genuine, lovable selves is true power. Shortly, you will learn how to dismantle your false self or your self-limiting beliefs in order to expand your authentic self.

Acceptance of yourself or of situations in your life does not mean you're resigned, helpless, or giving up. Actually, the opposite occurs. When we stand in acceptance, we free ourselves enough to ask, "What do I want to do now?"

Let me share with you a story about a Sea-Doo watercraft and a paddle. One gorgeous summer evening, back when I was still married, my husband and I found ourselves stranded in the middle of a lake in the Muskokas. We were cruising around on our Sea-Doo personal watercraft when it suddenly sputtered to a stop. We thought we were prepared by having our cell phones with us, but unfortunately, we didn't know anyone to call! This could have been a nightmare "blame-you" game if our old limiting beliefs had kicked in. I could have blamed my husband for not being more detail-focused and checking the machine out before we left and he could have blamed me for not wanting to go out earlier in the day, taking too much time to get ready for our ride, or whatever. Maybe the planets were aligned that evening or we were awestruck with the beauty of nature; fortunately, neither one of us were triggered. If one or both of us had been emotionally reactive, I guarantee one of us would have been swimming to shore. Instead, we accepted our reality, asked the question, "What do we do now?" and worked together. We assembled the small, portable paddle and began to head toward shore. It was dusk and the evening darkness was settling in—along with the mosquitoes. Two hours later, we arrived on the shore and tied our watercraft to a tree, hoping it would stay, and sheepishly approached a family eating a late dinner on their deck. Imagine two people popping out of the woods at night asking where they were. How crazy is that? Luckily, they didn't think we were axe murderers and offered to drive us back to our resort, about ten minutes away. With extreme appreciation, we offered to pay for the drive, but they would not accept anything. Today, we are still very thankful for these people who saved the day. Acceptance, plus a few deep breaths, goes a long way to keeping our triggers and overreactions to a minimum.

To accept ourselves and others, we have to practice compassion. There are many different definitions of compassion. For example, the Buddhist philosophy defines compassion as opening one's heart to the suffering of others and having the desire to help. Interestingly, it specifically refers to others. Developing feelings of warmth for ourselves is not a skill many of us were taught. It's easy to feel tenderness toward our children and partners, friends, and relatives. Why can't we do this for ourselves?

Steven Stosny, psychotherapist and author of several books, including *The Powerful Self*, suggests that individuals start with creating a list of characteristics they see in other lovable human beings. Seeing and identifying these qualities in yourself can be a daunting task so identifying them in others is often easier. Stosny noticed that when people do this task they often list various aspects of compassion. From this list, he recommends you choose the qualities that you have, too. Undeniably, you have some of those characteristics and need to acknowledge them.

I find as a clinician that people often have a misconception that if they're compassionate toward themselves they're being selfish or weak. Actually, this is a myth. Individuals such as Mohandas Gandhi, Mother Teresa, and Nelson Mandela were all compassionate, strong, and influential. Allowing ourselves to be self-compassionate not only increases our confidence, it also expands our ability to be creative and genuine and frees us of our shame. As well, we become genuinely compassionate toward others. Here are a few suggestions to build self-compassion:

- Surround yourself with people who are empathetic and kind. People who are content with themselves exude peace and compassion. They're like a breath of fresh air. Notice the type of people that drain you versus those that energize you. Make a conscious choice to increase your time with the latter.

- Choose environments that are conducive to cultivating compassion and goodwill. Such environments may include retreat centers, yoga centers, churches, or synagogues. Some individuals even create rooms in their homes where they are able to meditate or paint, listen to compelling music, knit, or sing. Be kind and compassionate to yourself by choosing surroundings that enhance your energy and revitalize you. If possible, decrease the amount of time in environments that deplete your energy.

• Learn to self-soothe. Healthy self-soothing ideas may include buying yourself a rose, preparing a gourmet dinner, sharing with a close friend, exercising, or experiencing a massage. Prepare a "warm and fuzzy" box filled with cards and notes from friends, lovers, and family members. When you're in a positive mood, write yourself a letter listing all of your strengths and the qualities that make you beautiful. Then, when you're feeling down or triggered by your LBs, read it over and over again. Dis-identifying from your self-limiting beliefs and shifting your thoughts to your true, authentic self is also part of compassion.

Embrace the Three C's: Feeling Connected, Capable, and Counted

One way to combat your coping styles and increase self-acceptance is to focus on the "3 C's," coined by Betty Lou Bettner and Amy Lou, authors of *Positive Discipline* and *Raising Kids Who Can*. The crucial C's consist of: the need to **connect**, the need to feel **capable,** and the need to **count**. When you feel connected, you feel secure and safe. When you feel capable, you feel competent, assume responsibility, and are self-reliant. When you feel that you count, you feel valuable and that you matter. Encouragement is the key to building the 3 C's within yourself and others. Practice encouragement by:

- *Recognizing effort and improvements.* Notice when you or your partner makes both small and significant shifts in behaviors. For example, if your normal reaction to criticism is to get defensive, give yourself credit when you do something different. This often empowers you to want to increase this behaviour.

- *Filling the holes versus finding the holes.* Notice the times when you or your partner are caring, considerate and patient. Or when you see him/her trying. Often, it is easy to minimize or pay no attention to these behaviors, and maximize mistakes. Of great importance in relationships is recognizing the strengths and talents you and your partner bring into your relationship. When you mesh your strengths as a team you experience partnership and a deep sense of belonging.

In order to enhance the 3 C's, you need to know when and where you feel capable and connected and that you count. The exercise below will assist you with this awareness.

3C'S EXERCISE

	Capable	Connected	Counted
Activities/situations that help you feel:			
People that help you feel:			

Now that you've looked at what assists you with the 3 C's, look at how you can help your partner feel capable, connected and that they count.

	Capable	Connected	Counted
Activities/situations I can create that helps my partner feel:			
Words and actions I can do that helps my partner feel:			

Lighten Up!

Have you become too serious as an adult? Did you know that children laugh up to 100 times a day and adults maybe 4 times? Increasing laughter decreases stress, increases cooperation, and improves communication. In our family, we made a point to cultivate laughter when life was beginning to drag us down. I remember one Halloween a few years back when my husband and I were married, we pulled a prank on our children who were now old enough to appreciate our teasing. One evening at dusk, we took the kids to a farmer's field to obtain cornstalks for decorating. Little did they know that we had planted a fake hand covered in blood, and a two-foot-long scary plastic rat, behind a clump of dirt. Our plan was to shine our flashlights on these gruesome things as we told them that this field used to be a cemetery. I had an ugly Halloween mask that I was going to whip on when they saw the fake hand. Our children saw the scary props in the earth, screamed, and came running towards me. I was laughing so hard I couldn't get the mask on. Imagine seeing this escapade: A psychotherapist running wildly around a corn field with four kids chasing her. By this time the kids had caught on, and they, too, were laughing hysterically, not believing their dull parents could plan such a trick. To this day, we still laugh as we reminisce together. There is nothing like laughing till you cry. My husband and I almost had as much fun planning this prank as we did carrying it out. Really, we are not sadists—we knew our kids also had a warped sense of humor and would handle it well.

Live by the Five Brainsense Principles

Our mothers didn't know the five Brainsense principles which can help anyone to let go of self-limiting beliefs and create better relationships. They are:

1. **Apply the 80/20 Rule**
2. **Change Unhealthy "Brainspeak" to Healthy "Brainspeak"**
3. **See the World Through Different Lenses**
4. **Pay It Forward**
5. **Entrain Your Brainwaves**

Paul and Cindy had only been married for two-and-a-half years and they either argued incessantly or ignored each other for days. They disagreed over money, their different parenting styles and their in-laws: three common stressors in a relationship. I knew the five Brainsense Principles could help them.

After Paul and Cindy had completed the self-assessment of their LBs (limiting beliefs) and coping styles (MASK), we sat down together to discover how these old patterns resulted in conflict. Paul's LB was that he was defective and the coping style he developed to deal with these negative feelings was the Actor, avoiding any feelings. He was usually out of their house and spent most of his time at his parents, playing sports or working at the office. Cindy's limiting belief was that she was alone and her coping style was the King/Queen, needing to control. Behaviorally, Cindy's need to control came out by telling Paul how to clean the toilets, dishes, and garage properly, how and when to spend money, and how to parent their little girl. Cindy had a strong need to be right and liked things to go her way. Paul was a perfect match for her initially because he was easy-going and avoided difficult feelings. Then, as time passed, Paul grew tired of being wrong all the time. He began to withdraw from Cindy, which contributed to her feeling more alone. A vicious cycle had evolved between the two of them and they both felt helpless and hopeless. Then Paul and Cindy began to focus on the five Brainsense Principles.

Brainsense Principle #1: Apply the 80/20 Rule

Paul and Cindy were introduced to the 80/20 rule. The 80/20 rule states that when we're triggered or emotionally distraught, 80 percent of our emotions come from our old LBs and 20 percent are rooted in present day reality. However, we experience 100 percent of the emotions and attribute these feelings to the present circumstances. In reality, only 20 percent of Cindy and Paul's emotions had to do with the issue at hand.

To apply the 80/20 rule, their first task was to become consciously aware of whenever their emotions began to escalate in discussions. Paul began to acknowledge to himself and to Cindy when he was feeling defective, whether it was feeling like he was a bad father, or husband. Cindy slowly learned to hear Paul when he voiced his fears, and decreased her control and criticisms. This was not an easy task for Cindy because often she was also triggered.

When both partners are triggered by their sabotaging beliefs, their thinking abilities significantly decrease. It's nearly impossible to have loving discussions when our emotions have hijacked us. I suggested that when both were triggered, they take a break in order to calm down, and realize that the intensity of their emotions were coming from their past history and old memories. I explained that both of them were responsible for "deactivating" their LBs (limiting beliefs), and they may want to initially do this apart from each other. As soon as they were both calm and rational, they could then come together again and discuss the issue at hand, keeping their emotions to a lower intensity. (When you take responsibility for your part in the conflict, even if it is recognizing that your LBs are triggered, your anger often decreases.)

With time, they both learned that their partner did not view them the way they viewed themselves. Cindy never felt or thought that Paul was bad or defective as a person (that was Paul's limiting belief) and Paul never saw Cindy as being different, abnormal, or a loner (that was Cindy's limiting belief). They were under the mistaken impression that their partner had the same feelings and perceptions about them that they did.

It is extremely important to examine reoccurring issues or problems to find some resolution. When we're experiencing only 20 percent of our emotional intensity, it's easier to discuss possible solutions. In counseling, Paul and Cindy were able to talk about a reoccurring situation they were not able to discuss at home because of their explosive emotions. The issue at hand was that at least once a week, Cindy would go out to bars with her friends where they would dance, and usually consume far too much alcohol, until 2:00 or 3:00 A.M. Cindy did this to try to relieve her feelings of loneliness. The morning after a night out, Cindy would wake up late and be cranky and impatient with their daughter. The old "forgive and forget" approach was not working for Paul.

When Cindy understood that her limiting beliefs were causing 80 percent of the intensity of her emotions, she became more accountable for her behaviors. She actually used her coping style of control on herself, significantly reducing her criticism of her husband. Cindy learned to find healthier methods of dealing with her loneliness. She also realized that blaming Paul for her feelings was only damaging their relationship. Yes, he was contributing to her feelings because he was avoiding interaction with her, but he was not causing her to feel alone. Cindy expressed to Paul that she would appreciate more alone time with him. She promised that the time they spent together would be enjoyable, that she would not use this time to talk continually about the problems in their marriage. The contentious issues were left for counseling sessions. She also agreed not to stay out so late and promised to have only one or two drinks when she went out with her friends.

Initially, Paul was resistant to her plan because he didn't want to give up any of his activities. Moreover, when they did spend time together, all Cindy wanted to do was talk about feelings or tell him all of his faults, so he wasn't certain she would carry through with her commitment to make their couple's time fun. When we looked at his weekly schedule, however, Paul realized that he was devoting only 2 to 4 hours each week to his wife and daughter. His need to keep busy outside of the house was coming from his fear of being defective as a husband and father. In reality, his coping style of avoidance (Actor) was only reinforcing his fear as he was neglecting his responsibilities. Like Cindy, he needed to admit to himself that it wasn't her fault that he was avoiding family time; he was doing it because of his old LBs and fears. Paul had to seriously ask himself if he wanted to hold on to his old coping strategies if it meant that he might lose his family.

With the 80/20 rule in mind, Cindy and Paul engaged in brainstorming ways they might spend more time together and made a list. Then they took turns crossing off options they didn't agree on. After looking at the remaining solutions, they decided to implement two of them for a month. At the end of the month, they would assess how this new commitment was working.

Over time, they learned to own their reactions and triggers, learned to be compassionate towards themselves and each other when they felt defective or lonely, and eventually found healthy coping strategies. They came to realize that becoming aware of old behavioral patterns and shifting them takes time and conscious effort. To their surprise, this awareness allowed them to stretch emotionally, grow up and push through old wounds.

Relationships that are abusive are a different story. Usually in an abusive situation, the abuser continually blames the other person and is not able to take responsibility for his or her behavior. The 80/20 rule doesn't apply as the abuser blames all of his or her pain on the partner. The partner who is accepting the abuse may need to leave, and seek couples or individual counseling.* Self-limiting beliefs can keep people in relationships that are not healthy.

The therapies I have found most helpful are EMDR (eye movement desensitization and reprocessing) and cognitive behavior therapy. (see Resources)

∞

Brainsense Principle #2:
Change Unhealthy "Brainspeak" to
Healthy "Brainspeak"

Another part of Paul and Cindy's homework was to identify their "Brainspeak": the negative self-talk that gets generated as a result of LBs (limiting beliefs). They listened consciously to their negative chatter when they were sad, frustrated, or angry and recorded these thoughts on paper. The following exercise guided them through this process. The knot and the infinity sign below are visual cues that may be used as reminders of negative versus healthy self-talk. The knot represents how our LBs tie us up. The infinity sign represents all the possibilities that come when we engage in healthy self-talk.

What's My Brainspeak?

Are you speaking from (limiting beliefs) or (reality)?

Situation/Event that triggered an emotional reaction.

Feelings and their intensity (Use a 0-10 rating scale, with 0 being low and 10 being high).

Write your version of what happened (for example, "How dare she blame me? She is such a jerk... After all I do for her!")

Which limiting belief was triggered: defectiveness, failure/not good enough, unlovableness, or alone-ness? How do you feel when you let the Brainspeak story go on and on?

What was your behavior in this situation you described? What did you do?

Imagine your limiting belief is gone. How would you feel about the same situation? How might you react differently?

What is your new healthy Brainspeak story? (for example, "I guess Cindy is having a bad day or she is also triggered. It has nothing to do with me being good enough or being a failure.")

Now that you are aware of the differences between feeling and acting from your old limiting beliefs, and acting consciously, which do you choose?

It's important to really feel the difference when you're acting from your old LBs and when you're not. Obviously it's unpleasant, anxiety provoking, and distressing to listen to your LBs. By contrast, it's quite freeing to listen instead to healthy Brainspeak, which isn't tainted by the old beliefs. Cindy mentioned that when her behaviors originated from her LBs it was almost like she was addicted to the negative emotions they generated. Some individuals subconsciously get an adrenaline rush from anger, stress, and frustration. Because of the familiarity of these emotions, they tended to be her habitual reaction. With time and conscious effort, Cindy was able to break this cycle and generate new behaviors and feelings.

If you focus on your feelings when you use the Brainspeak exercise, you will shift out of the old behaviors more quickly than if you just logically answer these questions. Scott Rabinette, General Manager of Hallmark Business Expressions, and Clair Brand, Customer Marketing Manager of Hallmark, have demonstrated that emotions stimulate the brain to work 3,000 times faster than regular thought alone! Feelings also allow you to tap into the unconsciousness which will help you more readily notice when you're operating out of old, limiting beliefs. Then you can choose to create new roadways in your brain and establish new patterns of thinking, feeling, and behaving.

Cindy's Brainspeak Exercise

Cindy recorded her Brainspeak, or negative self-talk, in her journal. She wrote:

Situation/event which triggered an emotional reaction:

Waiting for Paul to call.

Feelings and their intensity:

Angry (9 on 10 point rating scale); frustrated (8 on 10 point rating scale).

Write your version of what happened.

"Paul was supposed to call me and didn't. After an hour of waiting, I was angry and frustrated. He always forgets about me. How dare he ignore me? He never does what he says he is going to do. I feel like I have two children instead of one. He is the biggest jerk and the most disrespectful person I know."

Which limiting belief was triggered: defectiveness, failure/not good enough, unlovableness, or aloneness?

I am alone and can't count on others.

What was your behavior in the situation described? What did you do?

Ate chocolate, could not focus.

Imagine your limiting belief is gone. How would you feel about the same situation? How might you react differently?

I would feel lighter, happier, better able to handle the issue with more logic.

What is your new healthy Brainspeak story?

"Paul must have gotten caught in a meeting or maybe his cell phone died. I'm sure he'll call when he can. I think I'll go for a walk with my daughter, get some fresh air and sunshine."

When Cindy was caught in her negative chatterbox, she focused on what Paul didn't do, forgetting about the things he did do. Using words such as "never" and "always" makes the situation seem like a catastrophe. Name calling intensified her feelings and caused her to generate even more negative thoughts. The story she created in her mind made her feel angry, sad and discouraged. Cindy obsessed about her relationship with Paul, couldn't play with her daughter and resorted to eating chocolate. Then she would feel guilty for eating so much chocolate and blame her husband for her sweet tooth. She not only treated herself with contempt, but she would also blast Paul when he did call her, and refused to listen to his explanation. Cindy realized that her feelings of being alone and lonely were underlying her intense anger.

Then Cindy imagined that this LB (limiting belief) had vanished from her life. She would feel less anxiety and more peace, she would play and laugh with her daughter and would probably eat less chocolate. Without her LB, she would treat herself and others with warmth, playfulness, and love. Cindy laughingly said, "The kid in me wanted to rant and eat chocolate, but I told her lovingly that my adult part would take over, and she could just relax and play."

Cindy may still question why Paul was not able to call her, and might still need to ask him for more time together, but she wouldn't be as angry at him. Her ability to understand and listen to his perspective will significantly improve, possibly instigating tenderness from Paul. Dialoguing this way with her husband sets the stage for Cindy to potentially get her needs met— whether she needs a hug or reassurance that she's important to him and that he had no intention of hurting her feelings. Life would be totally different if she didn't hold on to her feelings of being alone. Cindy practiced the Brainspeak exercise for a month and realized that she's happier when she relinquishes her self-limiting beliefs.

Being freed from old patterns and the feelings they arouse in you is wonderful, but how do you accomplish this? The Brainspeak exercise assists you in becoming aware of your triggers, your behaviors, and your feelings. Awareness is the cornerstone of changing your old habits. Exploring your thoughts is an important step in this process.

Think About Your "Brainspeak"

**"There is nothing either good or bad,
but thinking makes it so."**

— William Shakespeare

Research demonstrates that recording any negative thoughts on paper helps people become more conscious of their thought processes, actually slowing down their automatic thoughts—what I call Brainspeak. David Burns, M.D., describes in his book, *Feeling Good,* that we can have thousands of negative thoughts per minute when we are stressed or anxious. No wonder we are so tired at the end of the day! Once we become aware of these thought patterns, we have more control over shifting them to more realistic, healthy thoughts. An important point to remember is that our self-limiting beliefs are not reality; they are distorted perceptions we hold in our unconscious memory banks. Our negative self-talk or Brainspeak can provide clues to the habits of thinking we learned as children.

I can remember giving my first presentation in front of a room full of psychiatrists, social workers, medical students, and the director of the hospital, who I perceived were noticing all of my errors and *umms* and *ahhhs*. It was paralyzing. I felt like a fruit fly under a microscope in a Grade 12 biology class. My internal self-talk (Brainspeak) was extremely negative, which accelerated my heart rate and blood pressure. I had a mental image of myself red faced, stuttering, and not making any sense at all. I was positive that they could see the perspiration marks under my arms. I felt like Colin Firth in the movie *The King's Speech*. My negative Brainspeak was sabotaging my presentation. I made it though the presentation and when my humiliation finally disappeared, I reflected on my thinking patterns. I decided that the next time I made a presentation, I would replace my limiting belief of "not being good enough" to doing my best because "my best is good enough." Changing my unhealthy Brainspeak to healthy Brainspeak allowed me to present keynote speeches with more ease.

Brainsense Principle #3:
See the World Through Different Lenses

It's crucial to understand that our old reoccurring patterns of negative thinking reflect a distorted perception of ourselves. To take a different perspective requires a conscious effort. If you think outside the box, you will be able to look at yourself differently.

The following exercise will help you learn how to switch out of your limiting beliefs and create a new pair of 'Brainsense sunglasses':

Sunglasses Exercise

Imagine you have a basketful of colored sunglasses with black, yellow, blue, and green lenses. When you put the black glasses on, you see the world through your limiting beliefs, such as, "I'm not good enough" or "I'm unlovable." Now put the red glasses on. With these rose-colored glasses, you see yourself and the world as totally perfect: Your children are perfect and so are your parents and your partner. The red glasses give you a perspective that's the opposite of the view through the black glasses. It's just another perspective. It's not any more real than when you look through your black sunglasses.

Next, place the yellow glasses on your nose. Through these lenses, you see yourself the way your best friend views you. If you're not sure of how he or she sees you, ask! Feel the love, pleasure, acceptance, and happiness your friend experiences when he or she is with you. Now view yourself and the issue you are dealing with through these glasses.

Next, put the blue glasses on. Through these lenses, you see yourself or the situation at hand in a totally logical way, facts only. For example, Cindy might tell herself that since Paul had a meeting with his boss, it's likely that he got held up and couldn't call her. Another fact she noted was that 85 percent of the time, Paul calls her when he says he will.

Finally, place the green glasses on and now see yourself with a fine balance of logic and emotion. Both have equal value. Once again, Cindy may acknowledge that she is feeling lonely and vulnerable because she has not heard from her husband; however, she'll be able to take responsibility for helping herself feel better. She may go for a walk or treat herself to a latte as she reassures herself that Paul doesn't deliberately neglect to call her and in reality, even if he didn't want to call her this doesn't make her unlovable or unimportant. Cindy's old coping style would be to jump into controlling behaviors and perhaps even call Paul and leave negative messages on his phone. The green sunglasses stopped her from her old habits.

The Sunglasses exercise trains your mind to see situations and yourself through different perspectives, which helps decrease the strength of your limiting beliefs, making it easier for you to choose to handle the situation in a more reasonable way. For fun, you may want to buy sunglasses with various colors of lenses and wear them to remind yourself that there are always different ways to see the world. Or, you might cut out photographs of sunglasses from magazines and stick them to your mirror or cupboards as reminders.

Perspective taking is a valuable asset in relationships as it expands our ability to understand our partner and lets us view situations from different angles or viewpoints. Individuals with high levels of emotional intelligence have the capacity to be aware of and regulate their emotions. With these traits it is easier to gain different perspectives, leading to creative solutions to problems or barriers. From my professional and personal experience, I believe that 75 percent of conflicts are due to individuals trying to convince their spouse that they're right and their partner is wrong. We fall into the trap of judging and criticizing, which only adds fuel to the fire. Imagine if you witnessed a car accident outside your office building or house. One person may see a tire fly off, another may see the windshield rupture and another may see the hood buckle. They're all correct perceptions and it would be a futile exercise to attempt to convince each other that the other person was wrong to have spotted something just because we didn't see it. Remember: *"We see things not as they are, but as we are."* The same goes in relationships. When we start to have a strong need to convince our partner that we're right, we're being triggered by our LBs.

Brainsense Principle #4:
"Pay It Forward"

"Simple kindness to one's self and all that lives is the most powerful transformational force of all."
– David Hawkins

To pay it forward entails two concepts: doing for others and feeling gratitude. Doing kind acts for your partner goes a long way to increase emotional intimacy or rebuild cooperation in a relationship. Often when a relationship is struggling, the partners go to their separate corners and either withdraw or come out with gloves up, ready for a fight. What would happen if you did the unexpected? What would happen if instead of fighting or withdrawing, you decided instead to reconnect and bought your partner his or her favorite treat or hired a babysitter so the two of you could go to a movie? What did you do when you first met? Did you send emails or texts daily? Did you go dancing? Nurturing and recreating these rituals in your relationship helps you get out of ruts. Stretching beyond your comfort zone, especially if you don't feel like it, demonstrates emotional maturity.

According to Jonathan Haidt, author of *The Happiness Hypothesis*, reciprocity or giving back is a deep instinct: humans do it naturally. If someone is kind or does something for someone our automatic response is to repay the favor. To enhance a relationship, the intention of rebuilding needs to be forefront in our minds, not the thought that, "If I do this, they'll do that." There has to be no strings attached. Reciprocity also helps to end conflicts. When you're able to apologize for your contribution to issues and conflicts, your partner is apt to reciprocate. As Haidt so eloquently says, "Reciprocity is an all-purpose relationship tonic. Reciprocity, like love, reconnects us with others."

Confucius, the philosopher and teacher, was famous for stating the Golden Rule: "Do not do to others what you do not want done to you." This was later translated into, "Do unto others what you want done to you." This ancient wisdom sounds so simple, but our old belief systems often become obstacles to practicing this Golden Rule.

I realize that sometimes we don't feel like being kind or considerate to our partners because we're angry and bitter about past events. Remember that 80 percent of your negative emotions are related to your LBs and 20 percent are related to your partner. You're responsible for dealing with your resentments and intense feelings. You can do this by practicing yoga, running, talking to friends, getting counseling, or meditating. All are viable options to reduce the emotional intensity of your feelings. Recognize that your partner or spouse's behaviors are also rooted in their limiting beliefs and old coping styles. This is not to excuse anyone's behavior, but understanding this makes it easier to view situations from different perspectives and not personalize others' action so much. Then you can resolve conflicts in a calmer manner.

The second part of paying it forward is gratitude, which has been touted by philosophers and Eastern religions for centuries. I was pleasantly surprised to learn that gratitude is supported by scientists and physicists as well. I have a dear friend in Pennsylvania whose husband was diagnosed with an inoperable brain tumor. He was fortunate to have had the best medical team supporting him. Paul went in for his appointment and was floored when his radiologist started talking about gratitude. This doctor adamantly told him to be grateful every day for what he has and that this would significantly help him through his radiation treatments. His gratitude and positive thoughts would help heal the tumor. Paul has now recovered and is working part-time, while appreciating every single day he's given. Gratitude allows us to notice and appreciate what we do have and to stop focusing on the things that make us unhappy.

One exercise I often give my clients is to write their own eulogy. How do you want to be remembered when you're gone? Writing your own eulogy can help you reflect on your priorities in life and lead to an increase in compassion and kindness towards yourself and others.

Brainsense Principle #5:
Entrain Your Brainwaves

Brainwave research has demonstrated that our brains produce different brainwave activities: beta, alpha, theta, and delta states. When we engage in our everyday activities, beta brainwaves dominate and we're alert, focused, and active. The alpha state occurs when we close our eyes, relax, or do a creative activity. Just before we fall into a deep sleep and just before we wake up, we're often in theta activity. This also occurs when we relax deeply or meditate. When we're in a deep sleep, we glide into the delta state. A healthy brain has the capacity to shift in and out of these states as the circumstances require. Researchers have categorized our brainwave activity into four different states based on their frequencies. Each brainwave state has a different function. They are as follows:

Beta   14-40 Hz   alert, focused

Alpha   8-13 Hz   relaxed yet aware, meditative

Theta   4-8 Hz   deep relaxation, "twilight state"

Delta   1-4 Hz   deep sleep

Brainwave entrainment gently guides your brainwaves to the desired brainwave activity (beta, alpha, theta, and delta) in order to relax, de-stress, sleep, or reenergize, enhancing emotional and physical health. Resting our brains is like refueling. Brainwave entrainment helps calm the brain's chatter so that you can become aware of your LBs and destructive thought patterns. Clearing the chatter also allows the brain to be in a more receptive state where you can then choose to create new conscious thoughts and behaviors. Clear thinking follows from the silence and often, solutions to problems emerge. Remembering and implementing the 80/20 rule becomes easier as your mind has had restful breaks.

The more you practice brainwave entrainment, the easier it is for your mind and body to achieve a meditative state. I had a client, I'll call her Natasha, bounce into my office one morning full of life. She had been using brainwave entrainment for two weeks and felt like she was a new person. Natasha had not had a full night sleep for over five years and was ecstatic because she had slept seven hour nights consistently. Her attitude about life had shifted from pessimism to optimism and hope. Previously, she described her mind as a prison cell, full of rampant, ruminating thoughts. Finally, Natasha said, she had found the golden key.

I'm in *awe* of how our brains work. In each brainwave state, the brain produces different neuro-transmitters that are important for both our mind's and body's health. Unfortunately, because of aging, stress, and diet, our brains often do not produce all the hormones and neurotransmitters needed for memory, learning, positive moods, sleep, etc. Brainwave entrainment enhances the production of these chemicals and slows aging, enhances memory, decreases anxiety, stress, improves sleep patterns, balances our appetites, and increases our overall emotional and physical health. For example, alpha brainwave entrainment increases the production of acetylcholine in our brain which aids our memory, plus it prevents the release of glucocortoids associated with stress and disease.

A research study done in December 2004 by Taheri, Ling, and colleagues published in the *Post Graduate Medical Education Journal* found that sleep deprivation was correlated with weight issues. Ghrelin and leptin are two hormones that balance our appetite. When we don't get enough sleep, the levels of ghrelin increase, activating our hunger and alternatively, the levels of leptin decrease which creates feelings of not being full. This research demonstrated that insomniacs were hungrier during the day which led to weight gain. To make it even worse, lack of sleep also leads to an increase in cortisol, leading to carbohydrate cravings: a double whammy.

Couples who use brainwave entrainment state that they feel more at peace and balanced in their lives. Their relationships improve, their joy in life increases and often, this peace enables them to discover the answer to some of life's bigger questions such as, "What's my purpose in life?" and "Why am I here?"

(For more information on brain entrainment, check out www.e-brainsense.com.)

Brainwave entrainment also improves your sex life which contributes to a healthy relationship. Simply put, brainwave entrainment improves your sleep patterns, which enhances your sex life. Does that seem like a contradiction? It isn't. Sleep is necessary for a healthy sexual libido. Monica Anderson, professor at the Federal University of Sao Paulo, spoke at the Fifth World Congress of the World Federation of Sleep Research and Sleep Medicine Societies, stating that sleep deprivation is causing lower sex drives in men and may also contribute to erectile dysfunction.

Women more typically have difficulties with sleep, which also affects their sex lives. A study done in 2007 by the National Sleep Foundation called "Sleep in America" revealed that 60 percent of American women have difficulties getting a good night's sleep. This sleep deprivation is not only causing poor quality of life such as sexual activity, it's also affecting women's health.

Sleep deprivation is becoming an epidemic in this fast-paced society. It harms our physical health and contributes to depression, anxiety, and mood swings. When we can't sleep, we have no energy for anything, including sex.

As previously mentioned, alpha, theta, and delta brainwave entrainment easily and effortlessly improves sleep patterns. Often, we cannot fall asleep because our minds are overly active and we're unable to lower our brainwaves from beta to theta, which is the first stage of sleep. Brainwave entrainment slows the brainwave activity, allowing us to gently slide into a deep refreshing sleep. When we feel refreshed and rested, our libido increases.

Make yourself a promise to practice the five Brainsense Principles for a six month period. I made this promise to myself and it transformed my emotional and mental health, allowing my intimate relationship to transform. Facing your LBs and old behavioral patterns eventually dissipates internal fears and anxieties. Confidence, compassion, and profound hope unfold, enabling you to communicate from your healthy needs and desires.

Make It Stick

Many of us have great intentions to change our behaviors when we read books like this one. Unfortunately, we get busy with our lives and forget all the effective strategies we learned. The suggestions below will help to increase your memory and allow Brainsense to become automatic. Obviously, it is more difficult to use Brainsense in the heat of the moment when you are angry, stressed, or sad. Creating daily reminders conditions your brain to remember, even when you're distressed.

1. *Visual Cues.* One way to remind yourself to use a technique you've found helpful, is to use visual cues, symbols, or signs to jog your memory. In the Brainspeak exercise, the knot and the infinity sign are visual reminders to notice when you're in your limiting belief story. Displaying pictures of sunglasses is a reminder to view yourself through different lens or perspectives. Do you remember when we first had to add area codes whenever we dialed telephone numbers? I was getting so frustrated hearing the recording say, "Please hang up and dial 613 before the number" that I put a red circle on my telephone at work. This visual cue reminded me to add the area code, decreasing my blood pressure!

    You can use recipe cards with key words, pictures, or abstract symbols. Place these cues on your mirror, refrigerator door, or telephone, or in your purse. After several days, change the locations or the actual symbol so you continue to see them. When the visual cues stay in the same location, they eventually become unnoticeable.

2. *Use the word STOP.* Say the word STOP out loud or to yourself—your brain seemingly responds to this word. I also encourage clients to wear an elastic band on their wrists and gently snap it when they say stop. This seems to snap us out of automatic habits.

3. *Daily Affirmations.* Daily affirmations are short positive statements you repeat to yourself as a way to decrease the intensity of your distorted negative thoughts and repattern your brain. Create a habit of practicing them when you open your eyes in the morning and before you fall asleep, whatever works best for you. Some examples may be:

- My heart and mind are filled with acceptance of myself.

- I am doing my best and that is good enough.

- I admire my ability to listen to others.

- I am not my negative beliefs.

- I deserve to be treated with respect by myself and others.

- I am lovable even if someone is disappointed in me.

4. *Remember Positive Memories.* Record specific examples and times when you felt positive, content, or successful. It can be as simple as having given your seat to an elderly individual on the bus, accomplished a goal or task, or achieved a high point in your life. When you start to tap into positive experiences, it's like your brain opens up a new channel and memories come streaming out. Describe at least five memories and focus on the positive feelings and thoughts associated with each one.

Positive Memory Exercise

Describe five situations/memories where you felt happy, successful, or on top of the world. Be specific.

i) _____

_____

_____

_____

_____

ii) _____

_____

_____

_____

_____

iii) _____

_____

_____

_____

_____

iv) _____

_____

_____

v) _____

_____

_____

_____

_____

Close your eyes and replay the memories in your mind. What are you doing? What are the feelings you are experiencing? Make the memory as real as possible using all of your senses.

_____

_____

_____

_____

_____

_____

Moreover, this exercise helps to reduce or counteract the negative memories that created and maintain your LBs. You've lived with the dull roar of negative memories in your conscious and unconscious mind for decades. It's time to right the balance. Reread these memories daily, allowing your brain to remember and refocus.

John Powell, author of *Happiness Is an Inside Job*, interviewed 100 of the most happy and successful individuals and found a common theme. Each of these people had the capacity "to look for and find what is good in him or herself, in others, and in all the situations of life." As you train your brain to remember positive moments and experiences, and not to ruminate about negative situations, you can decrease the frequency of your negative thinking and change your memory patterns. If you truly wish to change your relationships, you must change your thinking patterns.

Communicate with New Insights

Now that you understand self-limiting beliefs, coping styles and different strategies to shift your feelings and behaviors, I suggest you use these steps to change how you communicate.

1. **Remember the 80/20 rule.** Recognize when you've been triggered by your limiting belief and apply the 80/20 rule—80 percent of your feelings have to do with your old memories and patterns and 20 percent are related to your present situation. Reminding yourself of the 80/20 rule should start to decrease the intensity of your emotions and make it easier to communicate effectively.

2. **Stop an overly emotional discussion.** If your emotions are too intense to have a reasonable

discussion, express to your partner that you've been triggered and are not yet ready to speak because your old beliefs about not feeling lovable or good enough are influencing you. Then take a break to soothe your emotions using the Brainspeak exercise, the Sunglasses exercise, and/or brainwave entrainment.

3. **Depersonalize your partner's behavior.** When you're calmer, remember that if your partner is also triggered and reactive, he or she is speaking from limiting beliefs and coping with old behavior patterns too. This has nothing to do with you. Try not to personalize your partner's reactions.

4. **Set boundaries.** Set a boundary with your partner if he or she is overreacting. Explain that you would be happy to discuss the issue when your partner is calmer. Say something like, "I believe that our limiting beliefs are being triggered right now and we should take a break and discuss this when we're both feeling less emotional." Disengage! We never have effective communication when we're triggered.

5. **Start sentences with "I" not "you."** Often, we start our conversations with accusatory words such as, "You never tell me what your plans are for the week." This may contribute to your partner's defensiveness. To communicate more effectively, rephrase this sentence as, "I would like to plan our week's activities. When do you have time to talk about this?" Listen to your partner's responses and

feelings; do not interrupt. When you do discuss the issue, present your feelings and opinions from the 20 percent emotion spot.

6. **Stick to the issue at hand**. Do not bring up your partner's past mistakes.

7. **Brainstorm.** If a solution is warranted, try brainstorming viable options with the intent of reaching a win-win solution.

8. **Be patient with yourself and your partner.** Remember that you're breaking old habits and patterns, so be patient with yourself. Initially, when you start this awareness process, you may not realize you've been triggered until the next day or a few hours later. Then, with conscious effort, you will learn to catch yourself sooner and use the techniques more frequently. If you've diligently practiced these steps, and you or your partner are still having difficulties, counseling may be helpful.

9. **Are you in an abusive relationship?** If you're in an abusive relationship, recognize that shifting your LBs and coping styles may assist you in choosing to leave the relationship. People who believe that they're unimportant or not good enough may feel that they don't deserve more and they're willing to tolerate behaviors that are not healthy or appropriate. As well, the fear of being alone often prevents people from leaving abusive relationships.

Here Is What You Learned

- Simply put, we all merely do what we know, so start undoing what you know now!

- Change your brain. Replace negative Brainspeak.

- Practice acceptance and self-compassion.

- Embrace the Three C's. Recognize the importance of feeling connected, capable, and counted and work to make sure that you and your partner experience them.

- Lighten up! Humor can help minimize negative emotions.

- Live by the five Brainsense Principles:

  1. **Apply the 80/20 Rule**

  2. **Change unhealthy "Brainspeak" to healthy "Brainspeak"**

  3. **See the world through different lenses**

  4. **Pay it forward**

  5. **Entrain your brainwaves**

- Applying the Brainsense principles, making them "stick," is effective for breaking old habits that have prevented you from achieving rich, loving relationships with yourself and others.

∞

- Visual cues, affirmations, the word STOP and reliving positive memories will ensure the continual progression of transforming your negative habits into positive ones.

- Communicate effectively, using the principles and techniques you've learned.

AFTERWORD

EXCUSE ME, YOUR LIFE IS WAITING

"A journey of a thousand miles begins with a single step."
- Confucius

Congratulations! You have taken the journey. You've reexamined your belief systems and behaviors, and shed light onto those you didn't consciously choose in adulthood. Now you have the power to design the life and relationship you do consciously choose. Isn't it empowering to know that every decision you make from hereon in is not coming from old behaviour patterns you learned in the past – but from your new, enlightened self!

Remember the Talmud quote I stated in the beginning of my introduction – "We see things not as they are, but as we are..." By taking the journey you have just finished, and exploring your old behaviour patterns that were keeping you stuck and were sabotaging you from finding love – you have changed yourself forever. You have some new tools to continue your evolution into the person you have always dreamed of being – confident, joyous and your true authentic self!

As you have learned by changing your thinking, the past is exactly that – the past. And the future? The future holds unlimited possibilties thanks to your courage to let go of old behaviour patterns that were not working for you.

The time we have just spent together was one of inner exploration and awareness. You will now see that by freeing yourself of your old outdated ways of thinking and acting, you will naturally have more control over your thoughts, feelings, and behaviors. With this new awareness you can confidently create and enjoy the wonderful relationships you deserve.

My clients, who I see in my practice, and who I have introduced the Brainsense journey to are truly amazed at how life-changing this process is once they open themselves up to changing their thinking. If anything, they wondered why they didn't do it earlier! I tell them it all begins with their willingness to listen to themselves in order to unearth their own behaviour patterns that have been holding them back from finding love – and I know that this same process will work for you too! That is why I wrote *The Best Advice Your Mother Never Gave You* - to provide the inspiration and the tools that you will need to find love.

∞

My suggestion is that you keep coming back and reflect upon these pages again and again until it is second nature to you. The payoffs will be invaluable. For starters, as you begin to listen to yourself, others will also begin to listen to you in a whole new way.

We all have a desire to be happy and at peace – but where it gets tricky is when our desire to be happy and peaceful is buried by a mountainous weight of our self-limiting beliefs. When our self-limiting beliefs lurk beneath our consciousness it comes out "sideways" often in the form of anger, self-righteousness, jealousy or judgment. In using this book and starting to peel back your protective layers, your inherent connection with your inner strength and wisdom, which is your real self, is awakened. By arming yourself with Brainsense, you will choose (as in, no longer avoid) life-changing actions never before even thought of, much less attempted. Your life will literally catapult, right before your eyes! It is my most sincere wish that the healthy mojo within you has been reawakened and you're more than a little excited about your new discoveries and opportunities.

When you're invested in your own personal growth, that good energy can't help but spill over into other areas of your life, and your enthusiasm will influence those you love. With this awakening and awareness, you and/or your partner have a new and powerful language to communicate with, significantly reducing the emotional triggers, of the "he said/she said" games so commonly used in relationships. The five Brainsense Principles are the foundation of this new 21st century language which I hope you will continue to work with until it becomes second nature.

It is my sincere wish that this book's success is measured not only by the knowledge you have gained reading it, but also by how motivational it was to you for you to end up practicing and reaping the benefits of Brainsense. The unconscious mind's language is one of symbols and images. Therefore, keep in mind the images created in this book such as the infinity sign and the sunglasses, and perhaps the new symbols you invented – they'll assist you in making Brainsense more automatic. Remember it can take at least three weeks of consistent practice to change an old habit.

Make a commitment to yourself to stay excited and passionate about creating a healthy relationship with yourself and your partner. Ask people you trust to help you identify your old patterns when you get stuck. In doing so this can help remind you that your "black sunglasses" may be clouding the way you are seeing things. Sometimes we cannot see the forest for the trees.

There still will be challenging times. Rediscovery and awareness brings change and this isn't always comfortable for you or your partner. I urge you to not abandon the important changes you are trying to make in your life by running away from discomfort – but rather acknowledge your discomfort and then move forward with your new way of thinking! It is a normal part of the process to feel discomfort but your discomfort will fade once you experience the joy of using Brainsense.

Do not get discouraged if you revert back to some of your old triggers and behaviors. This too is a normal part of the process when you are trying to replace old behaviour patterns with new ones. Sometimes you may have to take two steps backwards in order to go one step forward. Be patient and have compassion towards yourself. If you are courageous enough to feel your discomfort and move through it you will end up feeling triumphant. You will begin to notice that the times of feeling discomfort will become less frequent and less intense – and just the fact that you are revisiting these old behaviors may be the very impetus you need to propel you forward even quicker as you remember how unpleasant it feels. You clearly see how these behaviors were not contributing to the life you truly desire.

Sometimes being uncomfortable leads to feelings of hopelessness and that all of our efforts have been in vain. When I've felt this way I reread a short inspirational story called *The Great Silent Grandmother Gathering* written by Sharon Mehdi. This enchanting story begins with two grandmothers who stand together in a park, quietly, not speaking at all.

They do this routinely every day. Soon the towns-people begin to talk.

Among them is a five-year-old girl who informs the citizens that these grandmothers are saving the world. This sends the townspeople further into a tizzy exclaiming, "The world doesn't need saving!" and "They're not even carrying banners or shouting slogans. Everyone knows you can't save the world without banners and slogans." But soon other women begin to join these two grandmothers - and by eight o'clock one morning, there are 2,223 women standing in the park. The local newspaper gets wind of this strange occurrence and writes a story. Hundreds of thousands of women start to gather in parks, forests, and fields across the continent. Now other newspapers from all across the world are writing about this strange phenomenon. Even more astonishing though, was the "unrelated story: it would appear there has been **no fighting** anywhere in the world today." In this story it took two grandmothers to start a ripple effect of peace – but the truth is that it only really takes one person. I hope it's you.

Once you increase your own self-knowledge and your excitement heightens, you may be itching for your partner to learn and grow as well. Sometimes with this keen passion, we get annoyed if our partner isn't interested. Your focus may then transfer to getting your partner onboard rather than freeing yourself from your own old behaviour patterns. Be cautious: It is a common human behavior to see the speck in our partner's eye yet miss the log in our own! As you know, the log is all of your old patterns that keep you stuck and stagnant in your life. Interestingly enough, once you deal with your log, your partner's "speck" sometimes disappears. Individual and/or couples counseling is at times needed to discuss patterns that don't seem to disappear.

However, if your tendency is to be critical of yourself, have compassion and patience as you embark on this new journey. Shifting your old behaviors often brings a sense of freedom and peace. Relationships grow and blossom and intergenerational patterns transform, allowing our children and our grandchildren to manifest a profound sense of connection in relationships.

I would like to end with a visual image. Imagine... every person is a unique piece of a puzzle which makes up the universe. Now imagine that each piece is connected, influenced, and dependent on all the others. Allowing our limiting beliefs to affect our communication with others affects the whole puzzle and throws everything out of alignment.

In order to complete the puzzle it is necessary that your part of the puzzle fits in place. That your limiting beliefs have been replaced with new beliefs which are representative of the person you are today. With these new beliefs you become aligned with who you really are and your puzzle piece fits into the big universal puzzle... the way it is suppose to.

Now that you have read *The Best Advice Your Mother Never Gave You*, you are ready to find love in the 21st century! I would love to hear all your success stories using the five Brainsense Principles.

Please write me at –
bestadviceyourmomnevergaveyou@gmail.com
Namaste

REFERENCES

Burns, David, M.D. *Feeling Good.* New York: HarperCollins Publishers, 1980.

Cialdini, Robert, Ph.D. *Influence: The Psychology of Persuasion.* New York: William Morrow and Company, 1993.

Collins, Jim. *Good to Great: Why Some Companies Make the Leap and Others Don't.* New York: Harper Collins Publishers, 2001.

DiAngelis, Barbara, Ph.D. *Real Moments.* New York: Bantam Doubleday Dell Publishing Group, Inc., 1994.

Haidt, John, Ph.D. *The Happiness Hypothesis: Finding Modern Truth in Ancient Wisdom.* New York: Basic Books, 2006.

Hanson, Rick, Ph.D. *Buddha's Brain: The Practical Neuroscience of Happiness, Love and Wisdom.* Oakland, CA: New Harbinger Publications, Inc., 2009.

Karpman, Stephen, M.D. "The Drama Triangle." Transactional Analysis Journal, 1970.

Katie, Byron. *Loving What Is.* New York: Three Rivers Press, 2002.

Kubler-Ross, Elizabeth, M.D., and Kessler, David. *Life Lessons: Two Experts on Death and Dying Teach Us About the Mysteries of Life and Living.* New York: First Touchstone Edition, 2002.

Lipton, Bruce, Ph.D. *Biology of Belief: Unleashing the Power of Consciousness, Matter and Miracles.* Santa Rosa, CA: Elite Books, 2005.

Mehdi, Sharon. *The Great Silent Grandmother Gathering.* New York: The Penguin Group, 2005.

Pennebaker, James, Ph.D. *Opening Up: The Healing Power of Expressing Emotions,* revised edition. New York: Guilford, 1997.

Powell, John. *Happiness Is an Inside Job.* Notre Dame, IN: Ave Maria Press, 1996.

Rabinette, Scott and Brand, Clare. *Emotion Marketing: The Hallmark Way of Winning Customers for Life.*New York: McGraw Hill, 2001.

Siegel, Daniel. *The Developing Mind.* New York: The Guilford Press, 1999.

Stosny, Stephen. *The Powerful Self: A Workbook of Therapeutic Self-Empowerment.* Germantown, Maryland: Compassion Power, 1996.

Schwartzer, R. Manage Stress at Work Through Preventative and Proactive Coping. In E.A. Locke (Ed.), *The Blackwell Handbook of Principles of Organizational Behavior*, Chapter 24, pp. 342-355. Oxford, UK: Blackwell.

Schwarzer, R. (1999b). The Proactive Attitude Scale (PA Scale). (Online). Available at: "http://userpage.fu-berlin.de/~health/proactive.htm"http://userpage.fu-berlin.de/~health/proactive.htm.

Taheri, Shahrad, Lin, Ling, Austin, Diane, Young, Terry, Mignot, Emmanuel. *Short Sleep Duration is Associated with Reduced Leptin, Elevated Ghrelin, and Increased Body Mass Index.* Post Graduate Medical Education. December 2004, no. 10.

RESOURCES

EMDR: The Eye Movement Desensitization Reprocessing Technique

Eye Movement Desensitization Reprocessing is an effective process for shifting old traumas and intense emotions. Francine Shapiro, Ph.D., psychologist and researcher, discovered EMDR in 1988. Many other researchers and clinicians have found that EMDR significantly reduces anxiety, depression, stress, post-traumatic stress disorder, trauma, and unhappiness. Certified EMDR therapists can guide you through the process.

NOTES

NOTES

NOTES

NOTES

NOTES

NOTES

NOTES

NOTES

NOTES

NOTES

NOTES

NOTES

NOTES

NOTES

CPSIA information can be obtained at www.ICGtesting.com
Printed in the USA
241038LV00001B/6/P